Three Notorious Female Politicians
in Feudal Japan

Three Notorious Female Politicians
in Feudal Japan

IIDA Yoriko

Osaka Metropolitan University Press

Title: Three Notorious Female Politicians in Feudal Japan

Author: IIDA Yoriko

Published on May 31, 2024 by Osaka Metropolitan University Press,
1-1 Gakuen-cho, Naka-ku, Sakai, Osaka 599-8531, Japan

Printed and bound by Ishikawa Special Express Binding Co., Ltd.,
7-38 Ryuzoji-cho, Chuō-ku, Osaka 540-0014, Japan

ISBN978-4-909933-74-4

Table of Contents

Introduction 1

Chapter 1: Hōjō Masako 11

Chapter 2: Hino Tomiko 43

Chapter 3: Yodo-dono 65

Conclusion 101

References 131

Introduction

In the world between in the late 11th century and the late 13th century, the crusader expedition started after the Pope's calling on people to recover the Holy City of Jerusalem from Muslim States. However, owing to many failings, the Catholic Church gradually lost its authority and the powers of the kings in some countries were getting stronger. During the 14th – 16th century Renaissance era, emphasizing the recovery of classical scholarship and arts, and respecting individual freedom without standing for the Catholic Church's point of view continued, developing astronomy and geography. Moreover, the Copernican principle prevailed. The compass, developed in China, was introduced to Europe by Arabian merchants visiting China. After the Ottoman Empire destroyed the Eastern Roman Empire (the Byzantine Empire) in 1453, it became a big country, controlling shipping routes in the eastern Mediterranean, which led to the Age of Exploration, enlarging the Spanish and Lusitanian culture. In Portugal, Bartholomew Diaz reached the Cape of Good Hope that was located at the southernmost point of Africa in 1488, which the Spanish Empire established in 1479. In Britain, the Tudor Dynasty came into existence and advanced oversees after the Hundred Years War and the War of the Roses. Europeans' discovery of new shipping routes and the overseas advance contributed to Asian trade, guns and Christianity being opened up to Japan. In the aspect of religion, there was transformative changes taking place in Europe. In 1517, the movement of religious reform by Martin Luther from Germany expanded to all over Europe and wars related to the religions occurred.[1] During this period a lot of innovative changes happened in the world.

---

1) Ōishi 2020, pp. 8–10.

Many changes occurred also in Japan. For example, in the Kamakura Era (1185 – 1333), the warrior came to mainly control the Japanese government instead of the emperor and noble families. In the Muromachi Period (1336 or 1338 – 1573), the Muromachi Shogunate lost its authority and Japan was led to the Age of Civil Wars (1467 – 1615)[2] when everything was confused and Japan was in chaos. After the Age of Civil Wars, Japan gradually began to create a new structure and supplanted the stable Tokugawa Shogunate.

In the transition period, three women were born. When the Crusaders went on expeditions in Europe, in Japan a woman whose name was Hōjō Masako was in the Kamakura Era, and in the age of the Renaissance another woman, Hino Tomiko was alive in the Muromachi Period, and in the Age of Exploration the third one, Yodo-dono existed during the Age of Civil Wars. The three women have been called *akujos* (bad women) in Japan from before, although it is not clear who began to say so. The Japanese people still seem to have acerbic images that they hold against them but why do they refer to them as *akujos*? Now Hōjō Masako and Hino Tomiko leave their names in a series of Atrocious People's Biographies and Yodo-dono's reputation is still not good. According to a Japanese dictionary, the definition of the *akujo* is the woman having an ugly face and being not good tempered. Were they actually so? This study examines their historical background and how they lived their lives, including Japanese cultural social backgrounds and analyzing whether they were actually bad women based on the criteria in the twenty-first century in Japan.

First of all, the research is going to briefly introduce the three women.

Hōjō Masako was the legal wife of Minamoto no Yoritomo[3] who established the Kamakura Shogunate, the very first warriors' government,

---

2) Regarding eras, there may be some different views.

3) The original *seiitaishogun* (Barbarian Subduing Generalissimo) at Kamakura Shogunate. It was the highest official position of warriors given by *chōtei* (a political organ whose top was an emperor and seized political power at that time).

and spent her life between the late Heian Period (794 – 1185)[4] and the early Kamakura Period (1185 – 1333). Actually, it is not clear that her first name was Masako because in those days it was common for women not to mention their real names in Japan. Takahashi says[5] that when she received a bureaucratic position from an emperor the first time, her name needed to be recorded and the name of Masako seemed to derive from Tokimasa, her father. However, it doesn't seem that she was actually called Masako by people in those days. She was born in 1157 but it is difficult to find written materials speaking about her childhood. The information about her was recorded after she married Minamoto no Yoritomo.

Around the time when she was born, the two families of the warriors, the Heike and the Genji, had large competing power in Japan. In the late Heian Period, two noblemen in *chōtei* had a battle and the Heiji War occurred. Both Taira no Kiyomori and Minamoto no Yoshitomo, Yoritomo's father took part in the war, and Taira no Kiyomori (the Heike Family, descendants of the emperor, Kanmu) defeated Minamoto no Yoshitomo (the Genji Family, descendants of the emperor, Seiwa) in the Heiji War. She fell in love with Yoritomo, being relegated to a district that was far from Kyoto, a capitol in Japan at that time, and married him while ignoring the objection of her father. The marriage was between a daughter of an unknown local strong man, a local official, and a son whose father was defeated and killed in the war. Before long Yoritomo decided to attack the enemy of his father with the Hōjō family, at last opening the Kamakura Shogunate. Masako always helped Yoritomo. After his death she entered a nunnery, supporting their first son, the second shogun, and their second son, the third shogun, as an examiner. After the two sons' death, she managed the government, taking care of an infant shogun from a court aristocracy in Kyoto. She was called an *amashogun* (a nun and shogun). She

---

4) There is a different opinion about the division of the generation. Some people say it was between 794 and 1192.
5) Takahashi 2004, p.2

won a power struggle against *chōtei* and made the warrior's government robust, helping her parent's families gain in authority. However, people called her an *akujo* since she had a strong desire for politics and a jealous nature due to destroying the residence where her husband's mistress lived.

Hino Tomiko was born in the current Kyoto Prefecture, Japan, in 1440. She came from a middle-class noble family and was a legal wife of the eighth shogun, Ashikaga Yoshimasa in the Muromachi Era (1336 or 1338 – 1573). The Ashikagas assumed the acceptance of girls from the Hino family as wives as a custom from generation to generation, and Tomiko married Yoshimasa at the age of sixteen. There is no clear record that she actually identified herself as Hino Tomiko and her authoritative name was said to be Fujiwara Tomiko[6]. In those days it was common for women to not disclose their real names to people except for special cases and they were usually called by their aliases (nicknames). What's more, because there is scant information related with women in ancient Japanese history, it is difficult to find the truth. Physically, she possessed long narrow eyes, a round face, a small mouth, and beautiful black hair. Yoshimasa was in possession of an exquisitely chiseled face with a strong, dignified nose. They were called "a beautiful woman and a handsome man."[7] Long narrow eyes, round faces, and small mouths seemed to be the qualities of pretty women at that time in Japan. However, she was notorious for being an "*akujo*", and was called "*shusendo*" (a miser), too. People said that she banished his concubines, controlled the government, and enriched herself off of heavily taxing people, lending money at high interest rates and so forth in order to increase her fortune.

According to the early chapter of *Ōninki* discussing the Ōnin War[8], in the course of the war, the shogun Yoshimasa had no interest in politics, which gave his wife (Tomiko), who did not have enough knowledge about it, the authority

---

6) Honda 1913, p.415.
7) Mitani 1994, pp. 8–10.
8) Shimura 2017, p. 12.

to manage the government. The author of *Ōninki* denies this behavior and the government being controlled by a woman.

Yodo-dono's autonym was Azai Chacha who was the eldest daughter of the three between Ichi, Oda Nobunaga's younger sister and Azai Nagamasa, *daimyō* (a feudal lord) in the Warring States period. Because of the wars she lost her mother and father, being brought up with her two sisters in the residence of Toyotomi Hodeyoshi. In due course, she became Hideyoshi's concubine, giving birth to two baby boys, Tsurumatsu and Toyotomi Hideyori. Although after Hideyoshi's death she managed the Toyotomi government in Osaka Castle, she killed herself with Hideyori there because of attacking by Tokugawa Ieyasu in Osaka Natsu no Jin (the Summer Siege of Osaka). Although in the paper the author is going to use the name of Yodo-dono, she was not always called so. She went by the names of Yodo no Nyōbō, at one period Ninomoru-dono, and Nishinomaru-dono, which are related to the name of the places where she lived.[9] However, because in the Edo Era someone began to call her Yodo-gimi, nowadays people in Japan are familiar with the name of Yodo-gimi. According to Tabata[10], around that time gimi meant the woman who prostituted herself. Someone might think that she was nothing more than a prostitute because young Chacha seduced old Hideyoshi, having him choose the wrong path, and destroying the Toyotomi administration. In essays not based on historical fact and non-fiction, she is often described as a sexually aggressive woman. Moreover, in them, she was described as a bad-tempered woman who was beyond control. Someone says because of her pride that did not accept Tokugawa Ieyasu's requests, the Toyotomi government was lost. It implies that since Ieyasu was at one time a subordinate warrior of Oda Nobunaga, her uncle, and Toyotomi Hideyoshi, her husband, she looked down on him.

The significance of presenting this topic is that it will contribute to developing history including culture and gender study, not only in Japan but all

9) Kuwata 1958, p. 3.
10) Tabata 2003, p. 80.

over the world because the work discusses the three women whose names have been left in Japanese history and people in Japan still refer to them as *akujos*. It is usually men, especially winners who are described as great persons in history but very few women left their names there. However, many Japanese people still know them as the legend. This means that focusing on them is important in the fields of history and gender study. What's more, it is meaningful to present medieval society, from the late Heian Era to the Age of Civil Wars, in Japan that was called the Dark Ages through their lives, since we can get hints at how other Japanese women survived and lived during the hard years. For example, all three women lost their husbands and children owing to disease and wars. Especially, Yodo-dono lost her parents, too. As there would be a great number of women having the same experiences as they had, we can imagine the many Japanese women who lived successfully despite their deep sorrows in those days. Before we go any further, we can't help but pay attention to the three women being active with their strong beliefs and living every day as best they could.

Problematic of other books discussing the topic, there are no works representing the three women together, neither in the Japanese language nor in English. However, there are some books talking about each person in Japanese although it is difficult to find any written in English.

Regarding Hōjō Masako, *Bakufu wo Seotta Amamidai, Hōjō Masako*, described by Tabata Yasuko and published by Jinbun Shoin, it is composed of seven chapters and talks about her whole life. Chapter 1 presents her marriage and her life after marriage; Chapter 2 introduces us to her life and her first son, Yoriie; Chapter 3 deals with her life and her second son, Sanetomo; Chapter 4 shows us her high social position including the Jyōkyū War; Chapter 5 describes her life after the Jyōkyū War; Chapter 6 mentions women in the warriors' world; and Chapter 7 speaks about her reputation. Nomura Ikuyo also discusses the life of Hōjō Masako, including her romantic love before marriage, her life and politics, her life as a nun and shogun, her relationship with Buddhism, and her reputation in her work, *Hōjō Masako Amashogun no Jidai*, issued by Kabushiki Kaisha Yoshikawa Kōbunkan.

Relating to Hino Tomiko, Mitani Masao mentions her life in his work, *Hyōden Hino Tomiko*, printed by Mainichi Shimbunsha. It presents Chapter 1, until marriage – successive shoguns and women in the Hino family; Chapter 2, a wife of a shogun – battles among women; Chapter 3, a ruler's loneliness – Yoshimasa and his times; Chapter 4, waiting on a baby boy – Yoshimasa's abdication from the position of shogun; Chapter 5, a maelstrom of war occurred – love affairs between Tomiko and the emperor; Chapter 6, woman calming the big war. Tomiko's astonishing technique of accumulation of wealth; Chapter 7, Yoshihisa's death – Ashikaga Family's disorder; and Chapter 8, Tomiko dies – the end of a government controlled by a woman. Moreover, Tabata Yasuko describes mainly the Ōnin War, Ashikaga Yoshihisa's life as a shogun, Yoshihisa's death, and her way of life in a section of work called, *Muromachi Shogun no Midaidokoro Hino Yasuko, Shigeko, Tomiko*, published by Kabushiki Kaisha Yoshikawa Kōbunkan.

As it pertains to Yodo-dono, Fukuda Chizuru speaks about her life in her work, *Ware Taikō no Tsuma to Narite, Yodo-dono*, printed by Kabushiki Kaisha Mineruba Shobō. It describes: Chapter 1, people around Chacha, Chapter 2, two boys' births, Chapter 3, she is called Mom, and Chapter 4, the end of Osaka Castle. Furthermore, Owada Tetsuo represents not only Yodo-dono but her two sisters in *Sengoku San Shimai Monogatari*, issued by Kabushiki Kaisha Kadokawa Shoten.

The products discussed above are interesting and beautifully achieve their purposes respectively: however, it is difficult to find a work talking about the three women together as the research mentioned before. Because the work deals with a long span of time between the Kamakura Era to the Age of Civil Wars, readers can historically understand how and when warriors' world in Japan began, evolved, and wound down, in addition to the transmission of women's social position. Furthermore, since a lot of famous warriors such as Minamoto no Yoritomo, Ashikaga Yoshimasa, Oda Nobunaga, Toyotomi Hideyoshi, and so forth in Japan related with the three women appear in the work, readers can briefly glean some information about the main warriors as well as the three women's lives. Finally, because there are no studies written in English, the work discussing this topic would help, not only experts and specialists but the general public all over the world who are interested in Japan, to access more knowledge about Japanese history, culture, people's way of thinking, gender studies, etc. Terminologies associated with the Japanese language are explained so that anyone can enjoy the product. The author would like to dig out Japanese topics that are still not written in English, introducing them to people in order to contribute to international cultural exchange.

The methodology of the work uses primarily Japanese primary and secondary sources as references, as it is neither a novel nor fiction but a research paper that should be historically accurate and get as close as possible to what was actually happening during a historical event. Regarding Hōjō Masako, as a main reference, the author accepted *Azumakagami*[11] which was written around 1300. It is a historical book composed with fifty-two volumes and the first record showing us the warriors' world, including basic information about the Kamakura Era. However, there are some views that unfavorable events and affairs for the Hōjō family were not presented, since the Hōjō family's persons in authority complied them. Since the book describes Masako after she became a legal wife of Minamoto no Yoritomo, there is no information about her childhood. Because of this, the study speaks about her after she became his wife. As they related to Hino Tomiko and Yodo-dono, owing to very few primary sources mentioning them, the author used Japanese secondary sources based on scholarly works explaining historical facts. These books are already introduced in the previous paragraph of other books relating to the topic.

The theoretical framework of the research is to discuss the relationship

---

11) Actually, the author used *Azumakagami* transcribed into modern Japanese (*Gendaigoyaku Azumakagami*) but the content is nothing different from the original one.

between a research question and its answers by examining the three women's historical, cultural, and social backgrounds. The research question is, "Hōjō Masako, Hino Tomiko, and Yodo-dono have been called *akujos* since the olden days in Japan although it is not clear how it began. Why and when did they begin to be referred to as *akujos* and are they actually awful women?" The answers of the research question are in the conclusion. Here, the paper presents what they mainly did in their lives as wives of top leaders, what jobs widows may have had after their husbands' death at that time, what reputations they had when they were alive, how women's social position changed, when it began to advance, and how people's way of thinking transmuted as time passed. After reviewing these criteria, the study will finally disclose whether they were *akujos* based on the mores of twenty-first century Japan.

The paper is composed of three chapters. Chapter 1 talks about Hōjō Masako, Chapter 2 discusses Hino Tomiko, and Chapter 3 presents Yodo-dono.

Chapter 1: *Hōjō Masako*

Hōjō Masako was born in 1157[12] as the oldest daughter of her father, Hōjō Tokimasa, living in Izu, the present Shizuoka Prefecture. She had three brothers, Munetoki, Yoshitoki, and Tokifusa, and two sisters, Awa no Tsubone and Tokiko. Her mother was not sure but people say she was probably a daughter of Itō Sukechika also living in Izu.[13] Both Hōjō Tokimasa and Itō Sukechika were part of the Heike Family, where Taira no Kiyomori enjoyed enormous authority in those days all over Japan. In 1177, when Hōjō Masako

Hōjō Masako

The seated statue of Hōjō Masako after she became a Buddhist priest.
It is owned by Anyōin, Japan. The image was obtained from Wikipedia in
accordance with the Creative Commons license attribution.

---

12) Tabata 2003, p. 16.
13) Ōtake 2018, pp. 165–166.

12

was in her twenty-first year, she married Minamoto no Yoritomo, he being in his thirty-first year, and became his legal wife.[14]

In 1147, Minamoto no Yoritomo was born as the third son of his father, a warrior, Minamoto no Yoshitomo,[15] who was killed after he got beaten by Taira no Kiyomori in Heiji no Ran (the Heiji War), beginning in 1159. Although Yoshitomo's first and second son were killed, the third son, Yoritomo was not killed but relegated from his district to Izu due to the help of Taira no Kiyomori's mother.[16] At first Itō Sukechika was told by the Heike Family that he needed to look after Yoritomo, whose situation was stable being a warrior leader's son in eastern Japan. He spent his young life praying for his dead family members in Heiji no Ran and sometimes enjoying hunting.[17] In addition, because of financial help from his foster mother and others, he had no financial problems although his life was not luxurious.[18]

In the Heian Era (794 – 1185) basically, the warrior was the servant of noble men who ran politics in Kyoto. When the warrior did a good job, such as squashing trouble in the countryside, he obtained a reward, like a high position in Kyoto[19] from the noblemen. While the noblemen at *chōtei* controlled politics peacefully, the warrior fought, thereby protecting the noblemen without involvement with the politics. However, warriors with high position enjoyed a life of luxury like that of noblemen and sometimes did put their nose into politics. Taira no Kiyomori was one of them. They were familiar with sophisticated culture and life in Kyoto. Minamoto no Yoritomo's father, a warrior who was a head of eastern Japan, also had a high position. This meant that Yoritomo was, in a way, a well-bred, graceful boy.

The origin of the warrior in Japan is not clear but there are two statements

14) Tabata 2003, p. 16.
15) He was a bosshead of warriors in eastern Japan. In those days, Taira no Kiyomori was powerful in western Japan.
16) Emiya 2022.
17) Azusawa 2017, p. 75.
18) Kaionji 1961, pp. 320–321.
19) A capitol of Japan in those days.

that have been found. One is that local farmers and local strong men armed themselves so as to keep themselves safe as in the middle of the Heian Era, the nation fell into decline and its public security worsened. The other is that in Kyoto, there were noblemen of low class whose regular vocation was military arts to protect the emperor from danger, maintaining public order around Heian Castle. Probably the two strong families of the warrior, the Genjis (Minamoto) and the Heikes (Taira) were from the latter. The warrior was a pit bull of the *chōtei* and their social status was low. Some warriors from the local people were barbarian and rough, and it was not always warriors that contributed to the *chōtei.*

In the world of the warrior, the one with a high position had residences in both his hometown and Kyoto where he usually lived. He went back and forth between the two residences. Minamoto no Yoshitomo, Yoritomo's father, and Taira no Kiyomori were such warriors having high positions from *chōtei.* On the other hand, subordinate warriors lived in their hometown, working for their master without directly relating with *chōtei.*[20]

Before long, Minamoto no Yoritomo became a young man, falling in love with the third daughter of Itō Sukechika, Yae. In those days Itō Sukechika was leaving his home in order to work at Kyoto for three years. The next year when he left his home, Yoritomo and Yae were blessed with a baby boy. He was named Senzuru and everyone was very happy. However, Itō Sukechika returning home never allowed their marriage to go forward because he took the side of the Heike Family. He then did not accept the young man from the Genji Family, forcing them to get a divorce and killing their son by drowning him in the river. He also got his daughter to marry a different man, trying to kill Yoritomo.[21]

Fortunately, Yoritomo was saved and Hōjō Tokimasa took over Itō Sukechika's job, working as a watch dog and helping Yoritomo. Soon Masako

20) Itō, 2021, p. 481.
21) Ibid. pp. 321–322.

and Yoritomo fell in love with each other. After learning of their association, Tokimasa was afraid of retribution from the Heike Family too and tried to make Masako marry someone. Tokimasa had her tie the knot with the man under duress. However, in the middle of the night on her wedding day, she ran away in torrential rain to a shrine at Izu Mountain. Although women were usually not able to reach there on foot, Masako made it. Masako and Yoritomo lived together on Izu Mountain for a while then secretly.[22]

In times to come, Masako gave birth to a baby girl Ōhime in 1178. After learning of Masako's pregnancy, her father Tokimasa changed his mind, accepting Yoritomo. Then the relationship between Tokimasa and Yoritomo improved and they came to trust each other, keeping a good master-subordinate relationship. Tokimasa always supported Yoritomo as a senior subordinate warrior.[23]

In April, 1180, Yoritomo was in Hōjō's residence and received Mochihitoō's order to hunt down and kill the Heike Family.[24] Yoritomo showed people in eastern Japan the order from Mochihitoō and insisted on his authority of conducting politics there. Yoritomo left Masako and some female servants supporting her at a shrine in Izu, promising he was going to donate some land to the shrine after the war settled down. Yoritomo asked Masako and the servants to do daily devotional exercises for him, and he went to the war front.[25]

First Yoritomo's army attacked the residence of Yamaki, a minister of Izu[26] from the Heike Family at night and destroyed it, however six days later they got terribly defeated at Mt. Ishibashi. Although Yoritomo went missing for a while, soon he appeared and took numerous armies that were against the Heike Family

---

22) Kaionji, 1961, pp. 323–324. Gomi & Hongō, 20, June, 2008, p. 41.
23) Tabata, 2010, p. 94.
24) Gomi & Hongō, 10, November, 2007, pp. 2–3. Mochihitoō was the third son of the emperor, Goshirakawa.
25) Tabata, 2010, p. 94.
26) Yamaki is a person Masako were forced to marry before mating with Yoritomo.

to Kamakura,[27] a stronghold of the Genji Family in eastern Japan, the current Kanagawa Prefecture. Masako seemed to receive this information from her father and Yoritomo.[28] In Kamakura, Yoritomo began to build his residence and another for his daughter, Ōhime, as well as setting up Tsurugaoka Wakamiya, now Tsurugaoka Hachimangū (a shrine)[29], around 1181.[30]

Masako grew ill in December, 1181, and many subordinate warriors of Yoritomo gathered together around their residence.[31] Masako seemed to be a *midaidokoro* who was respected and loved by the warriors since she supported Yoritomo and his warriors during the war. Her illness was mental exhaustion due to the war and heavy emesis of pregnancy. She had an obi-wearing ceremony to pray for the safe delivery of the baby with Yoritomo's help on March 9th. The baby was their second one and everyone was so happy. Owing to this happiness, Yoritomo also started civil engineering work for a road between Tsurugaoka Wakamiya and a beach to be made direct, praying for the safe delivery. Masako's father, Tokimasa and warriors carried sand and dirt.[32]

In July, 1182, Masako moved to a residence at Hikigayatsu for the delivery[33] and gave birth to a baby boy whose name was Yoriie on August 11th.[34] Since around the time of the delivery was a do-or-die job and a big public event for the Minamotos, some subordinate warriors worked for it as one of their public duties. A lot of warriors in the Kantō area also looked forward to the coming baby.[35] The daughter of Yoritomo's foster mother[36] also became one of Yoriie's. Many warriors made Yoriie presents of swords and horses. On the 17th of October, Masako and her son, Yoriie left the residence of Hikigayatsu

27) Kamakura was (is) in the current Kanazawa Prefecture.
28) Kaionji, 1961, p. 326.
29) Guardian gods for Kamakura warriors are enshrined.
30) Tabata, 2003, pp. 20–21.
31) Gomi & Hongō, 10, November, 2007, p. 95.
32) Watanabe, 1961, pp. 25–26.
33) Nomura, 2000, p. 15. Gomi & Hongō, 10, November, 2007, p. 111.
34) Watanabe, 1961, pp. 28–29.
35) Tabata, 2003, pp. 22–24.
36) Awa no Tsubone.

16

for their home with their servants.[37]

Although Yoritomo was mindful of Masako's well- being, he was not able to be satisfied with only one wife. Before marrying Masako, Yoritomo had relations with Kamenomae who was not a woman with a high position but was meek and gentle. In June, 1182, Yoritomo called her over to his house. After Masako returned to her home with the baby boy, he still continued seeing her. On November 10, Masako heard about this from Maki no Kata, her mother-in-law from the Maki family and became extremely angry.[38]

Because Yoritomo was brought up in Kyoto, a capitol of Japan, and was familiar with the life of noblemen who experienced romance in daily affairs, he didn't think much of monogamy. However, Masako grew up in a farming village in the countryside, and it was a convention of sound village life, so polygamy was never allowed without her severe remonstrance.[39]

Masako ordered Maki Munechika to destroy the residence of Fushimi Hirotsuna where Hirotsuna hid Kamenomae and he moved to the housing of a warrior. The day after, Yoritomo visited the warrior's housing, bringing shame on Munechika by cutting his fixed hair.[40] Yoritomo said, "It is solemnly that you think much of *midaidokoro* (Masako), however, you should have told me that before you conducted the affair." The Maki family was furious after learning what Yoritomo did. Because Masako's mother-in-law was from the Maki family, Masako's father Tokimasa disapproved, coming back to Izu from Kamakura. However, relations between Kamenomae and Yoritomo still continued, even with her fear of Masako. Yoritomo did not allow Kamenomae to leave him. On the 16th of December[41] finally, this case had a strange outcome. Although Fushimi Hirotsuna was a supporter of Yoritomo, he was transferred to a local district and demoted by Yoritomo due to Masako's extreme

37) Gomi & Hongō, 10, November, 2007, pp. 115–116.
38) Gomi & Hongō, 10, November, 2007, p. 116.
39) Watanabe, 1961, p. 28.
40) In warriors' world, long hair was justifiable and short hair was shameful.
41) Gomi & Hongō, 10, November, 2007, p. 119.

displeasure.[42] It would seem that Yoritomo was not able to defeat his wife and his father-in-law in the end.

Although what Masako did might have come from her fiery temper, it also had a connection with a social convention called *uwanariuchi* in the Heian Era (794 – 1185). For example, a legal wife sometimes burst into the house of her husband's mistress with her support group and rampaged the mistress's house. Alternatively, the mistress sometimes took them on too. The husband needed to take responsibility for his illicit affair but the legal wife hated the mistress. Without repressing her hateful feelings she was allowed to express them in a socially institutionalized way. However, such a thing did not always happen. This custom continued at least until late in the Muromachi Era (1336 or 1338 – 1573) in some regions. Regarding Masako, she did not hurt Kamenomae directly but destroying the house of Fushimi Hirotsuna might be associated with the custom.[43]

In addition to Kamenomae, on July 14,[44] 1182, Yoritomo also sent a love letter to a widow, an ex-wife of his elder brother through Fushimi Hirotsuna when Masako was pregnant. The widow didn't accept Yoritomo's love and her father helped her daughter marry someone else. Because of this, Yoritomo's romance was not successful, and Yoritomo kicked her father out. After that, Yoritomo again and again had mistresses, and every time Masako grew very angry.[45]

In 1183, before Minamoto no Yoshinaka from the Genji Family, who had already defeated many Heike members in the Hokuriku region,[46] went to Kyoto in order to attack Heike members there, he sent Yoritomo his eldest son, Yoshitaka, as a captive so as to keep a good relationship with Yoritomo. Yoritomo accepted his son and decided to have his oldest daughter, Ōhime, also

---

42) Tabata, 2003, pp. 25–26.
43) Nomura, 2000, pp. 17–18.
44) Gomi & Hongō, 10, November, 2007, p. 111.
45) Kaionji, 1961, p. 329.
46) Current around Toyama, Ishikawa, Fukui, and Niigata Prefectures in Japan.

marry him in the future. Yoshitaka was eleven years old and Ōhime was five or six years old at the time.[47]

In Kyoto, Yoshinaka knocked down Heike members, running from Kyoto in July. Furthermore, Yoshinaka make a foray to the west. However, Heike members in Shikoku and Kyūshū were very strong and Yoshinaka was given a hard time. Moreover, he failed in having people in *chōtei* take his side because he was unable to make a success of the political negotiation with the emperor, Goshirakawa, a father of Mochihitoō who ordered Yoritomo to defeat the Heike Family. Since Yoshinaka attacked the housing of the emperor, Goshirakawa incarcerated him, and he lost support from both noblemen and warriors.[48]

The movement of Yoshinaka triggered an increase in Yoritomo's power in eastern Japan so that it would now extend to all parts of Japan. Yoritomo sent his army whose heads were his younger half-brothers, Minamoto no Noriyori and Minamoto no Yoshitsune to Kyoto,[49] and they had a battle with the army of Yoshinaka so as to save the emperor, Goshirakawa. Although Yoshinaka held the position of *seiitaishogun,*[50] he was killed by Ishida Jirō, a warrior. At last, the army of Noriyori and Yoshitsune rescued the emperor, Goshirakawa. In February, 1184, it fought with Heike members of Ichinotani, in the existing Hyōgo Prefecture, beating them, although Heike's power was recovered for a while after Yoshinaka's death. What's more, in February, 1185, the army of Noriyori traveled to Bungokoku, Kyūshū[51] to fight with Heike members there, defeating them. In addition, the army of Yoshitsune headed into Sanukikoku, Shikoku in February too[52] in order to get on top of Heike members in the area. Finally, in March, the Heike and Genji armies met in Dannoura, in the current Yamaguchi Prefecture.[53] They had a battle and the Genji army rode to victory.

---

47) Watanaba, 1961, p. 33.
48) Gomi & Hongō, 1 March, 2008, pp. 14–15. (introduction)
49) Ibid. p. 5.
50) Ibid. p. 3.
51) Ibid. p. 74.
52) Ibid. p. 76.
53) Ibid. p. 87.

The Heike Family ceased to exist and the war between the Heikes and the Genjis was over. The foundation of the government all over Japan controlled by Minamoto no Yoritomo was established. Actually, in Kamakura he had already set up *samuraidokoro* in 1180,[54] and *kumonjo* and *monchūjo* in 1184.[55] He then founded the Kamakura Shogunate and was assigned to be a *seiitaishogun* by *chōtei* in 1192.[56]

Around the time when the war between the Heikes and the Genjis was over, the relationship between Yoritomo and Yoshitsume was getting worse and worse. Yoshitsune had an excellent achievement in the war. However, Yoritomo did not like him because Yoritomo's warriors told him that Yoshitsune had received a bureaucratic position from the emperor, Goshirakawa, without Yoritomo's permission[57] and that Yoshitsune acted on his own authority during the war.[58] In May, 1185, although Yoshitsune explained his innocence to Yoritomo in a letter,[59] Yoritomo did not accept it. In October, 1185, after receiving the rumor that Yoshitsune might betray him, Yoritomo ordered his warriors to avenge him.[60] In November, *chōtei* were also ordered to hunt down and kill Yoshitsune.[61] In July, 1186, Yoshitsune's secondary wife, Shizuka gave birth to a baby boy but he was killed at sea.[62] On 22 May, 1189, Yoritomo

---

54) Gomi & Hongō, 10, November, 2007, p. 56. *samuraidokoro*—government of subordinate warriors, military affairs, and the police.
55) Gomi & Hongō, 1, March, 2008, pp. 53–54. *kumonjo*—financial administration. *monchūjo*—court cases.
56) Gomi & Hongō, 10, March, 2009, p. 153.
57) Gomi & Hongō, 1, March, 2008, pp. 48–49. Yoshitsune did not ask the emperor, Goshirakawa to give him the bureaucratic position. The emperor, rather, gave it to Yoshitsune because he did a very good job.
58) Ibid. pp. 98–99. The exchange between the warriors telling Yoritomo that Yoshitsune acted on his own authority during the war was probably not wise. The warrior might lie in envy of Yoshitsune owing to his great achievement. Yoritomo should not have only accepted the warrior's opinion.
59) Ibid. pp. 111–114.
60) Ibid. pp. 136–137.
61) Ibid. pp. 152–153.
62) Gomi & Hongō, 120, June, 2008, p. 76.

20

received the information that Yoshitsune had been killed on April 30th.[63] The housing of Yoshitsune was attacked, and he and his family were killed.[64]

Regarding Minamoto no Yoshitaka, Ōhime's fiancé, Yoritomo was planning to kill him because his father was put to death after betraying the emperor, Goshirakawa. In April, 1184, the female servants of Ōhime received this information and relayed it to her secretly. After receiving it from Ōhime, Yoshitaka ran from his housing on a horse disguising himself as a female servant. Un no Yukiuji, Yoshitaka's friend, helped him. However, at night this escapade came to light and Yoritomo was very angry, holding Yukiuji under arrest. Yoritomo ordered his guards to find and kill Yoshitaka. Because of the situation, Ōhime became confused.[65] At once Yoshitaka was caught to be killed by Tōnai Mitsuzumi, Yoritomo's subordinate warrior at Irumagawa, the present Saitama Prefecture. Although this affair had been a secret from Ōhime for a while, she soon discovered it, refusing to eat because of her deep sadness. Masako and many servants felt sympathetic toward Ōhime and were lost in melancholy.[66] In June, Tōnai Mitsuzumi held an execution by Yoritomo, though Mitsuzumi just followed Yoritom's order and was not wrong, all because of Masako's strong grievance related to Yoshitaka's death. After Yoshitaka's death Ōhime was sick, getting worse and worse both mentally and physically. Masako said, "Mitsuzumi should have told Ōhime about Yoritomo's scheme. Why didn't he do so?" Masako was so angry that Yoritomo was not able to save Mitsuzumi.[67] In 1186, Ōhime stayed at Shōchōjuin (a temple) in Kamakura

---

63) Gomi & Hongō, 20, September, 2008, p. 74.
64) Yoritomo had strong suspicions because he had been relegated to Izu and brought up thereunder surveillance. He always thought that he should be suspicious of people.
   After he defeated the Heike Family, his suspicions were getting deeper. As he might always fear losing his top position, he was careful with even his brother or people from the Genji Family. As a result, he did a grave disservice to his half–brother, Yoshitsune, as he killed him. Yoshitsune, without his great achievement of defeating Kiso Yoshinaka and the Heike Family in Dannoura, Yoritomo could not have established Kamakura Shogunate. However, it was Yoritomo that cemented his name in Japanese history, not Yoshitsune.
65) Gomi & Hongō, 1, March, 2008, p. 33.
66) Gomi & Hongō, 1, March, 2008, p. 35.
67) Ibid. p. 43.

for two weeks to emotionally heal from the trauma, however, she never fully recovered.[68]

As the paper mentioned before, Yoritomo was not satisfied with only one wife in his life. Around 1191, Daishin no Tsubone was his public concubine and bore a baby boy, Jōgyō. She was a warrior's daughter and a servant of Kamakura Shogunate.[69] Because on a daily basis Yoritomo was familiar with both his male and female servants, they seemed to be close. The relationship between them became public knowledge in eastern Japan after she gave birth to the baby.[70] Masako felt so bad about it because she did not know about it. Yoritomo, who was afraid of Masako, sent Daishin no Tsubone to Kyoto, helping her get income from Ise no Kuni, the existing Mie Prefecture that was near Kyoto.[71] Although he tried to find a nanny for their son, many people did not accept the position since they were very much afraid of Masako. Finally, Nagato Kagekuni was assigned to take the job.[72] Later Jōgyō was sent to Ninna-ji (a temple), in Kyoto in order to become a monk.[73]

Masako again had a baby on the way. In April, 1192, Yoritomo told a monk to pray for her easy delivery every day, taking care of Masako.[74] Although he had various types of affairs with a lot of women, he was nice to Masako during her pregnancy. On August 9th, a baby boy, Senman (later, Sanetomo) was born. Many people rushed to Masako to celebrate his birth.[75] They also commemorated the 6th and 7th day after he came into the world.[76]

With the first son of Masako and Yoritomo, Yoriie, he was in his twelfth year in 1193. In May, for the first time, he shot a deer with his subordinate

---

68) Gomi & Hongō, 20, June, 2008, p. 50.
69) Gomi & Hongō, 10, March, 2009, p. 97.
70) Tabata, 2003, p. 97.
71) Gomi & Hongō, 10, March, 2009, p. 97.
72) Ibid. p. 147.
73) Ibid. p. 152.
74) Ibid. p. 146.
75) Ibid. pp. 158–159.
76) Ibid. p. 160.

22

warrior's help during the hunting. Yoritomo then gave up hunting because he was so happy and held a festival representing thankfulness toward God. Yoritomo also sent his warrior to Masako in Kamakura to tell her about his achievement. However, she did not think it worthy, saying, "It is not so important an event. I take it for granted that Yoriie, a warrior, hunts a deer. You don't have to come all the way from your place to tell me such a thing."[77]

According to Tabata, someone points out that the event shows Masako's low political status against Yoritomo's high one. In 1192, Yoritomo was assigned *seiitaishogun*, the top of all the warriors in Japan, wanting to show people that his political heir, Yoriie was also great and deserved to take over his position controlling all parts of Japan. On the other hand, Masako seems to treat Yoriie as a successor to a common warrior without envisioning him as a shogun in the future.[78]

In July, 1194, Ōhime was sick again but in August she recovered a long way for a while. Then Masako tried to help her marry Ichijō Takayoshi, a nobleman, when she was in her seventeenth year. However, she rejected it, saying, "If I have to enter into another marriage, I'm going to kill myself." After receiving this message, Takayoshi declined to tie the knot with Ōhime.[79] In 1195, because she was again in poor condition, a monk prayed for the removal of her negative energies, and she made a recovery. Yoritomo was very happy.[80]

In 1195, Yoritomo visited Kyoto with his family so as to take part in a memorial service[81] at Tōdai-ji (a temple) in the existing Nara Prefecture.[82] The true purpose of his visiting there was to send Ōhime to the harem of the emperor, Gotoba.[83] Masako and Yoritomo approached a woman,

77) Gomi & Hongō, 10, June, 2009, pp. 14–16.
78) Tabata, 2003, pp. 54–55.
79) Gomi & Hongō, 10, June, 2009, p. 52.
80) Ibid. p. 109.
81) A service for reconstruction of the Great Buddha.
82) Gomi & Hongō, 10, June, 2009, p. 74.
83) Nomura, 2000, p. 33.

Tangonotsubone[84] who had a large influence in political circles in Kyoto. At that time, although the emperor, Gotoba in his sixteenth year, already had two wives, Masako and Yoritomo still tried to send their frail daughter to his harem in Kyoto which was very far from Kamakura. They thought that it would be the happiest life for a woman to give birth to an emperor's baby, especially a boy. However, in 1197, Ōhime passed away before entering the harem. Masako's distress and sinking sense of disappointment was beyond description, saying that she wanted to cross the veil with her although Yoritomo did what he could to comfort her.[85]

The unhappiness of Ōhime began when she became a princess of Minamoto no Yoritomo, head of all warriors in Japan, as her short life was always related to politics. The position of princess was useful to the Minamoto Family to keep good relationships with Yoshinaka, a member of the Genjis, a nobleman, and an emperor. But it meant that her life needed to follow Yoritomo's agenda focusing on a rising social position. If she were not his daughter, she might have had a happier life.[86]

Masako and Yoritomo had another daughter whose name was Sanman, being born in 1186.[87] After Ōhime passed away, they again tried to send in Sanman to the harem of the emperor, Gotoba.[88] However, she too breathed her last breath before entering the harem. Tanba no Tokinaga, a good doctor from Kyoto, took care of her initially[89] and she got back on her feet for a while, being able to eat regularly. Everyone was happy. However, by and by she again developed the eccentric condition with her eyes getting swollen. Tokinaga then said it was hopeless, saying that he could no longer help her anymore.[90] On June 30, 1199, she went to heaven, which had Masako feeling immensely sad.

---

84) Nomura, 2000, p. 89.
85) Ibid. pp. 34–35.
86) Seki, 2004, pp. 17–18.
87) Ibid. p. 23. Sanman was commonly known as Otohime.
88) Nomura, 2000, p. 35.
89) Gomi & Hongō, 10, June, 2009, p. 117.
90) Ibid. p. 121.

She was buried at a chapel on the estate of Fjiwara no Yoshichika, a husband of her foster mother. On July 6th, her memorial ceremony was held.[91]

In January 1199, Yoritomo passed away. Although the cause of death was, someone says, falling from a horse, it is not clear because not enough sources of the information exist. Masako was so sad, saying that she wanted to die following her husband. However, when she thought of her children, she was not able to do so because it would be so terrible for them to lose both parents at the same time.[92] On March 2nd, a memorial ceremony of the 49th day after his death was held.[93] After his death, Masako entered a nunnery.[94]

Yoriie in his eighteenth year at that time, the first son between Masako and Yoritomo, took over Yoritomo's position. On March 5, 1199, Yoriie took Gotō Motokiyo's position on the grounds of perpetrating a crime. So that instead of him, Kondō Kunihira took over the position.[95] On April 1st, Yoriie decided to go to trial, not in the shogunate focusing on fairness, but out of it.[96] The shogunate saw what Yoriie did as tarnishing the good relationship that Yoritomo and his warriors had set up, and denied him. It was decided on April 12th that Yoriie would not be allowed to get a word in with a trial and that court cases would be judged by thirteen warriors with high positions.[97] Yoriie was not permitted to take any court cases on his own behalf.

Moreover, the shogunate had a problem with Yoriie's behavior. On

---

91) Gomi & Hongō, 10, June, 2009, p. 122.
92) Nomura, 2000, pp. 55–56.
93) Ibid. p. 116.
94) At that time it was common for a wife to enter a nunnery after her husband died. In addition, in the observance of those days, lots of people became Buddhist priests after the death of their respectful person.
95) Gomi & Hongō, 10, June, 2009, p. 116.
96) Ibid. p. 118.
97) Ibid. p. 118–119.
Thirteen warriors were Hōjō Tokimasa (Masako's father), Hōjō Yoshitoki (Masako's brother), Ōe Hiromoto, Miyoshi Yasunobu, Fujiwara Chikayoshi, Miura Yoshizumi, Hatta Tomoie, Wada Yoshimori, Hiki Yoshikazu, Adachi Morinaga, Adachi Tōmoto, Kajiwara Kagetoki, and Nikaidō Yukimasa. People say that Masako seemed to associate with the event on the 12th of April. Masako, having more power than Yoriie after Yoritomo's death, began to control the shogunate with her Hōjō family, including her father and brothers.

July 16, 1199, Adachi Kagemori left for Mikawakoku, in the present Aichi Prefecture, in order to settle a dispute, although he firmly declined the job at first. He did not want to separate from his secondary wife in Kyoto for a moment, however, he had to do his duty. After Kagemori's leaving, on the 20th Yoriie had his subordinate warrior take Kagemori's secondary wife to the warrior's house so as to make love to her. Although Yoriie sent love letters to her before, she never said "Yes". For this reason, Yoriie ordered his warrior to do so using his authority. Later, Yoriie had her move to a place near his location and only five warriors who were his favorites were allowed to visit the place. In August because a taleteller told Yoriie that Kagemori held his secondary wife against Yoriie, he ordered the five men to kill Kagemori without making sure of the truth.

After getting this information, through her servant Masako told Yoriie, "Because your father and sister recently passed away, we are in the middle of grief. If you fight with him, it would be the cause of wild times. Kagemori is a good man and was trusted by Yoritomo. Can you give me all the details? I'll take care of it. Without making sure of the truth, you would regret it in the future. If you still hunt him down and kill him, kill me first before doing that." Finally, Yoriie begrudgingly gave up defeating Kagemori.[98]

On the 20th of August, Masako also visited Kagemori's residence and advised him, "This time I was able to stop Yoriie's flagrant behavior. But in the future when the same thing happens, I don't know I would be able to deal with it because of my old age. How about writing Yoriie a letter that you are not against him?" Kagemori soon followed her advice. Masako went home and showed his letter to Yoriie saying, "You tried to kill Kagemori, which was so unthoughtful and inhumane. The defensive action in the shogunate was not enough and you think light of the politics without considering your people. You are a womanizer, ignoring their reproach. Regarding your servants, they are not

---

98) Gomi & Hongō, 10, June, 2009, pp. 122–125.

26

wise, just flattering you with lip service. Warriors are your father's family and the Hōjōs are my relatives. While your father always cherished the Hōjōs, you look down at them without giving them any reward, calling them under their own name.[99] They feel upset at this disrespect and might be against you. Make a cool-headed decision about everything, then you will not have to fight with them, keeping the peace.[100]

Although Yoriie was not allowed to judge court cases, there was a warrior asking his advice on territorial boundaries. The territory was very important and the issue related to a significant shrine of the *chōtei*, however Yoriie drew a line in the center of the territory on a map irresponsibly saying, "The person with luck will get the bigger portion. We need neither to send delegates there to examine the situation nor to judge it. It is a waste of time."[101] Furthermore, Yoriie suddenly had a notion to give some territory to people unrelated to the situation. His warriors persuaded him to give up this idea, suggesting, "Such a thing has never happened before and people would come down hard on it."[102] Because the issue of land was the most important for people of that time, it needed to be decided through court, based on the fairness that the Kamakura Shogunate thought so much of. Owing to his irresponsible, immature decisions, acting without first considering the politics of the situation, people gradually drew away from him.[103]

Yoriie indulged playing with the *temari*[104] ball after the emperor, Gotoba sent Kinai Yukikage, a super performer of the *temari* ball to Yoriie

99) In those days calling people under their own name was impolite. They should be titled.
100) Gomi & Hongō, 10, June, 2009, pp. 125–126. What Masako wanted to say is to keep a good relationship with warriors serving the shogunate since if Yoritomo was alive and treasured them, then you would not fight with them, the shogunate keeping a stable condition. Only Masako gave Yoriie such severe criticism because she was his mother having the same authority that Yoritomo had. She needed to lead Yoriie in the direction that was the best for his becoming a successful shogun.
101) Gomi & Hongō, 10, June, 2009, pp. 150–151.
102) Ibid. pp. 159–160.
103) Yoriie did not have enough capability as a head of the government.
104) It is a ball whose exterior has pretty designs.

in September, 1201.[105] Then he played with it each and every day. Hōjō Yasutoki[106] told Yoriie's close advisor, "It is good for Yoriie to be interested in the *temari* ball because it is a subtle and profound entertainment. However, last August because of big gale the gate of Tsuruoka Hachimangū (a shrine) was destroyed and people still suffer from famine." In the face of that situation, he called over the performer and enjoyed the *temari* ball on consecutive days. "Moreover," the advisor went on, "a while ago we had an extraordinary natural phenomenon occur. Yoritomo, now deceased, refrained from playing on the beach and prayed for people's safety when the extraordinary natural phenomenon occurred. How about advising him to understand the situation?" Although the close advisor well understood what he said, he was not able to relay this to Yoriie. Later, Yoriie got the information from someone else and got angry.[107]

On January 29th, 1202, Masako also admonished Yoriie, "Refrain from the *temari* ball because one of our important old warriors passed away on January 14th. If you go to play with the ball, people will blame you. We should mourn." Yoriie argued back, "There is no relationship between people's blame and the *temari* ball," he gave it up. He was not able to cross his mother with authority.[108] However, Masako had sometimes visited Yoriie to take part in a banquet of kicking the *temari* ball.[109] On July 22nd Yoriie was appointed to become a *seiitaishogun*.[110]

The following year a doomful divine revelation was told to Ichiman, the son of Yoriie, in Tsurugaoka Hachimangū. An oracle said, "An unexpected affair will occur this year. Ichiman will be unable to take over his father's position because a stool of a tree on a bank had already rotted. However,

---

105) Gomi & Hongō, 10, November, 2009, p. 12.
106) Hōjō Yoshitoki's first son, a cousin of Yoriie.
107) Gomi & Hongō, 10, November, 2009, pp. 14–15.
108) Ibid. pp. 20–21.
109) Ibid. p. 23, 25. Masako called on Yoriie's palace to participate in a banquet of kicking *temari* ball on March 15th and June 25th.
110) Ibid. p. 27.

nobody recognized it, waiting for green grass."[111] This might drop a hint that Yoriie would fall from his position.

Around the summer of 1203, Yoriie fell sick again and was getting worse and worse[112] although in March he had been sick and recovered.[113] According to *Azumakagmi*,[114] this year he went to Itō and the foot of Mount Fuji with his servants to explore the caves there, killing a snake.[115] After that, strange happenings occurred. For example, his servants died and pigeons in Tsurugaoka Hachimangū were found dead. Then Yoriie became sick.[116]

On July 27, with Yoriie in critical condition, the shogunate decided to divide his territories toward Ichiman, his first son, and Senman, his younger brother.[117] Ichiman was in his sixth year, Senman his twelfth year, and Yoriie twenty second year. However, Hiki Yoshikazu, Ichiman's grandfather on his mother's side did not like that Senman received the territories, too. Actually, he wanted his grandchild to get all of them and control the government on the pretext of supporting Ichiman. Because of this reason he tried to kill Senman and his relatives.[118]

The big battle between Hiki Yoshikazu, Yoriie's father-in-law and Hōjō Tokimasa,[119] Yoriie's grandfather seemed to start when Hiki Yoshikazu secretly told Yoriie, being sick in bed, that they should defeat Tokimasa. At first Yoriie was surprised but almost agreed with him. However, Masako

---

111) Gomi & Hongō, 10, November, 2009, p. 33.
112) Ibid. pp. 40–41; July 23, August 7, & August 27.
113) Ibid. p. 36.
114) Ibid. pp. 38–40; June 1, June 3, June 30, & July 9.
115) There was a folklore that the snake was an envoy from God. If people killed it, terrible things would happen to them.
116) Back in those days people believed in hauntings and what the diviner said. People usually acted after choosing a good day. Some Japanese calendars still present when is a good day, when is a bad day, and others.
117) Gomi & Hongō, 10, November, 2009, p. 41.
118) Ibid. p. 41.
119) After Yoritomo's death, the shogunate was mainly controlled by Masako and the Hōjō family as Yoriie did not have enough ability to manage the government. Because Hōjō Tokimasa was Masako's father and he held actual power, he was targeted.

caught the information in the clandestine meeting behind closed doors. She soon sent a messenger to let Tokimasa know. After being sad and thinking a lot about it, Tokimasa sent Hiki Yoshikazu a message saying, "I'd like to invite you to our Buddhism service and I want to talk to you about various matters on the occasion." Yoshikazu accepted the invitation. Yoshikazu's relatives advised him, "Be careful. How about arming yourself?" But he went without arms. Tokimasa and his warriors bearing arms were waiting for him to kill him. Yoshikazu's servants ran away to tell the Hiki family and they locked themselves in the residence of Ichiban. Masako sent the army to destroy them. One of the warriors in the army set fire to the residence, everyone there including Ichiban were burned. Furthermore, people from the Hiki family who were still alive after the battle also meted out punishment.[120] Without Masako's message to her father, a big war involving many warriors all over the country would have occurred due to the issue of dividing territories.

Although Yoriie was a little recovered, he was very sad and angry after receiving the information that his son and the whole Hiki family were murdered. Then he ordered his servant to put Tokimasa to death. However, the servant was killed, too and Yoriie experienced more strain of grief than before. On September 7, 1203, Yoriie became a Buddhist priest on Masako's order, although actually, he did not want to do it.[121]

On November 6th, Masako received a letter from Yoriie.[122] It said, "I'm very bored because I'm in the mountains without any entertainment. Can you send my servants who have supported me for a long time? In addition, can you tell Adachi Kagemori[123] to visit me? I want to place sanctions on him."

---

120) Gomi & Hongō, 10, November, 2009, pp. 42–46.
121) Ibid. pp. 46–47. Masako recognized that Yoriie might be a hazard to the government because he was sick and lacked the capacity as a shogun. He was sent to a temple whose name was (is) Shūzen-ji in Izu, in the current Shizuoka Prefecture.
122) Seki, 2004, p. 98. Gomi & Hongō, 10, November, 2009, p. 54.
123) Adachi Kagemori is a person who was taken his secondary wife by Yoriie.

However, Masako did not accept his favor and Yoriie was prohibited from even sending a letter to her. His servants were relegated to a place that was too far from Kamakura.[124] On July 18, 1204, he passed away in the temple in his twenty-third year.[125]

After Yoriie retired, Senman (after his coming-of-age ceremony, then called Sanetomo), the second son between Masako and Yoritomo, succeeded his position[126] and he received appointment as *seiitaishogun* in September, 1203.[127] He was in his twelfth year. Soon Sanetomo moved to the housing of Hōjō Tokimasa, his grandfather. However, because Awa no tsubone, Masako's sister and Sanetomo's foster mother, told Masako that she should not trust Tokimasa's second wife, Maki no Kata, as she seemed to have a plot against them, and Sanetomo might be in a dangerous situation there, Masako decided to have him in her residence for his upbringing.[128] On October 8th, Sanetomo's coming-of-age ceremony was held and people celebrated him.[129] The shogunate did common people in some parts of eastern Japan a favor by cutting their tax in November[130] and in December, hunting by a governor of each district was prohibited by Masako in order to protect farmers from harm, given by the governors' hunting.[131]

After Sanetomo's ceremony, his next task was to decide his lawful wife although he was still in his thirteenth year. On August 4, 1204, subordinate warriors of Sanetomo had a meeting to discuss the issue. Although a daughter of Ashikaga Yoshikane[132] was floated as a top candidate, Sanetomo did not

124) Gomi & Hongō, 10, November, 2009, pp. 54–55.
125) Gomi & Hongō, 10, November, 2009, p. 66. A view is that Yoriie was killed by the Hōjō family.
126) Ibid. pp. 47–48. Because Senman was still a child, Masako and Tokimasa always supported him, controlling the government.
127) Ibid. p. 49.
128) Ibid. p. 48.
129) Ibid. p. 50.
130) Ibid. p. 56.
131) Ibid. p. 57.
132) Ashikaga Yoshikane, a warrior, always took the side of Yoritomo since Yoritomo had set up the Kamakura Shogunate. Masako and others trusted this, keeping a good relationship with

accept her, saying that he'd like to welcome a daughter of a court noble, Bōmon Nobukiyo[133] from Kyoto. Sanetomo decided how many men and who was going to meet and welcome her at Kyoto.[134] On October 14th fifteen warriors left Kamakura for Kyoto to pick her up.[135] On December 10th she arrived at Kamakura.[136]

In June 1205, the following year after Sanetomo entered into a marriage, Maki no Kata talked to her husband, Hōjō Tokimasa about killing Hatakeyama Shigetada and his son, Hatakeyama Shigeyasu. Her reason was that Shigeyasu spread false information about Hiraga Tomomasa, a husband of Maki no Kata's daughter, so as to frame Tomomasa.[137] Although Tokimasa held counsel with Hōjō Yoshitoki and Hōjō Tokifusa, his sons, they did not trust the reason presenting. They said, "Because the parent and the son were very loyal and Shigetada is your daughter's husband, we should not act hastily without making sure of the truth." Then Tokimasa withdrew. However, since Maki no Kata insisted that it was true, Yoshitoki believed what she said. The next day a lot of soldiers rushed to Yuiga beach[138] after getting the information about killing betrayers. Hatakeyama Shigeyasu also came on the run. Then Shigeyasu was killed there and Shigetada was murdered on his way to Kamakura, too.[139]

However, it was soon perceived that Hatakeyama Shigeyasu was innocent and never knew that he was a target to be killed. Hōjō Yoshitoki felt sorrow

---

him. Also, Masako's sister married Yoshikane. However, regarding a marriage between the warriors, there was a danger that a war over the shogun's position might occur like in a case with Yoriie's father–in–law. What's more, in order to have people again recognize that the position of a shogun was higher than those of any other warriors, and that the shogun was totally different from other warriors although he was a warrior too, Sanetomo should marry a daughter of a noble man whose position was higher than that of warrior.

133) An uncle on the maternal side of the emperor, Gotoba.
134) Gomi & Hongō, 10, November, 2009, p. 67.
135) Ibid. p. 69.
136) Ibid. p. 71.
137) Around that time, giving the wrong information to set someone up was a heavy offense.
138) Yuiga beach was(is) in Kamakura.
139) Gomi & Hongō, 10, November, 2009, pp. 76–79.

giving way to tears and his father, Tokimasa said nothing.[140] The fact was that because Hiraga Tomomasa bore a grudge against Hatakeyama Shigetada, he told Maki no Kata, a second wife of Tokimasa the wrong information that Hatakeyama Shigetada had concocted a treason. After Tokimasa found out, he secretly spoke to Inage Shigenari about the issue. Since Inage Shigenari told Hatakeyama Shigetada that they needed to kill betrayers at Yuiga beach, Shigetada rushed there. After everyone knew the truth, there was no one who did not lament.[141]

It was Masako who needed to do the post-handling of the affair because Sanetomo was too young to deal with it. Masako passed on Hatakeyama's territory to people with achievements in a fight and rewarded her female servants for their help.[142] This job was usually done by a shogun. Since it was an absurd affair at that time and difficult for Sanetomo, who did not have enough political experience to cope with the issue, Masako worked for it. Although Sanetomo was a shogun with a wife, and only at the age of thirteen, Masako always supported him.

On July 19, 1205, Masako received the information that Maki no Kata was plotting to kill Sanetomo in her home because she wanted Hiraga Tomomasa, her daughter's husband to become a shogun. After discovering this, Masako soon told her subordinate warriors to take him from Maki no Kata's residence to that of Hōjō Yoshitoki, Masako's brother. On the same day, Hōjō Tokimasa suddenly became a Buddhist priest as did many other warriors. He was in his sixty-eighth year. The next day Hiraga Tomomasa left Kamakura for Izu. Hōjō Yoshitoki took over his position and became a regent. On July 26th Hiraga Tomomasa was murdered.[143] On January 6th in 1215 Tokimasa breathed his last

---

140) Gomi & Hongō, 10, November, 2009, p. 80.
141) Ibid. p. 80.
142) Ibid. p. 81. The territory of a betrayer was always taken, to pass it on to warriors with achievements in battle.
143) Ibid. pp. 81–82.

breath because of cancer.[144]

Because Sanetomo was a little fragile, Masako was usually anxious about his physical condition. There are records that he was actually sick on July 14, 1204,[145] November 3, 1204,[146] April 13, 1207,[147] February 3, 1208,[148] April 11, 1208,[149] June 2, 1211,[150] and August 10, 1215.[151] Regarding February 3, 1208, he was sick with smallpox. Although he recovered, he was never the same. Because Masako was worried about him, on October 10th Masako went forth to shrines in Kumano, in the current Wakayama Prefecture with her servants[152] so as to pray for his perfect recovery. After spending three months, on December 20th, they came back to Kamakura.[153]

Sanetomo liked learning, being good at composing the *waka* (Japanese poetry). He liked study and read a book whose name was *Jōganseiyō* when he was nineteen years old.[154] The book from China was a text book for learning how to be a good shogun, mentioning questions and answers about politics. Regarding *waka*, he sent his works to Fujiwara no Sadaie[155] in order to receive corrections from him.[156] Sadaie gave *Manyōshū*[157] to him, which made Sanetomo very happy saying it was the most important treasure for him.[158]

---

144) Gomi & Hongō, 10 April, 2010, pp. 14–15. It is said that Masako had Tokimasa become a Buddhist priest and sent him to Izu because he was always an order–taker of his young second wife, Maki no Kata, without thinking much of politics.
145) Gomi & Hongō, 10 November, 2009, p. 66.
146) Ibid. p. 70.
147) Ibid. p. 99.
148) Ibid. p. 107.
149) Ibid. p. 109.
150) Ibid. p. 146.
151) Gomi & Hongō, 10 April, 2010, p. 18.
152) Gomi & Hongō, 10 November, 2009, p. 115.
153) Ibid. p. 118.
Sanetomo usually kept up a good relationship with Masako unlike Yoriie because his foster mother was her sister and the Hōjō family devoted a lot of attention to him.
154) Ibid. p. 147.
155) In those times Fujiwara no Sadaie (Teika) was a famous poet.
156) Ibid. p. 122.
157) It is the oldest poetry book compiled in between the late 7th and the late 8th century in Japan. It contains 4,500 poems whose authors are from emperors to farm people.
158) Ibid. p. 225.

34

Sanetomo seemed to prefer literary to military arts. On September 19, 1213, the knowledge that Hatakeyama Chōkei (a monk), the youngest son of Hatakeyama Shigetada was planning to rise in rebellion was reported. Sanetomo told his subordinate warrior to catch Chōkei and bring him to Kamakura. However, the warrior killed Chōkei and brought back his head[159] to Kamakura. Sanetomo deplored him, saying, "Shigetada was murdered in spite of his innocence. It was in haste that Chōkei was killed without making sure of the situation." The warrior retorted, "Because his high treason was certain, I sent him to eternity. If I brought him to Kamakura, he would be saved owing to allegations of Masako and her female servants.[160] Since I guessed so, I ended him. When Yoritomo was alive, he had a hash attitude toward rebellions. However, you like literary better than military arts. We should focus more on military arts as warriors."[161] Although Sanetomo seemingly was judicious, he might not have been good enough as a warrior of the day.

On January 27, 1219, a cruel affair in which Sanetomo was killed occurred. On this day he paid his respects at Tsurugaoka Hachimangū (a shrine) with many of his subordinate warriors after receiving a higher position from *chōtei*. When he was leaving the shrine, Ajari Kugyō,[162] Yoriie's son, a monk, rushed at Sanetomo to wipe him out.[163] His warriors tried and failed to catch Kugyō. Then Kugyō sent a messenger to Miura Yoshimura[164] to tell him, "Now the

---

159) In Samurai world, bringing back someone's head was common in order to prove the person's death.
160) After Yoritomo's death, Masako enjoyed huge political power. Not only Yoriie but Sanetomo seems not to have been against her.
161) Gomi & Hongō, 10 November, 2009, pp. 221–222.
162) Masako took Kugyō under her wing because he was her grandchild. When he was a child, she had a ceremony for him in her residence. She also had Sanetomo accept Kugyō as his privately adopted child without the right of taking over Sanetomo's position.
163) His legal wife entered a nunnery and many warriors servicing with Sanetomo became Buddhist priests because they were not able to bear the suffering from his death.
164) Because Miura Yoshimura was Kugyō's foster parent, his son was also a monk in the same temple and Yoshimura had power to defeat the Hōjō family, so Kugyō asked him to assist him. However, Yoshimura did not accept Kugyō, holding back tears and told the truth to Hōjō Yoshitoki. Kugyō seemed not to be a gentle monk in his life.

shogun has disappeared. I (Kugyō) am going to be the next shogun. Please support me." However, Yoshimura told this to Hōjō Yoshitoki, a regent. He immediately ordered Yoshimura to kill Kugyō. Although Kugyō was good at military arts and it was difficult to murder him, finally he was deceased. Masako also ordered her warriors to completely destroy Kugyō's gang.[165]

Actually, before visiting Tsurugaoka Hachimangū on January 27th, Sanetomo left his death song: "Even if a master (Sanetomo) managing flowers on the Japanese apricot trees in his garden passes away, he would like them to open up without forgetting spring."[166] What's more, he pulled out a strand of his hair and gave it to his servant saying, "It is my memento."[167] Did he foretell his own death?

Masako had no time to wallow in misery because the government needed to decide the next shogun very soon. Unfortunately, Sanetomo had no heir. After due consideration, the shogunate decided it would like to have a member of the Imperial Family from Kyoto. Masako[168] sent her messenger to chōtei, advising, "We would like to have Rokujō no Miya or Reizei no Miya as our next shogun."[169] However, the grand emperor, Gotoba did not give the messenger a clear answer, saying, "This is acceptable but not now..."[170] On March 9th the messenger of the grand emperor, Gotoba arrived at Kamakura, presenting that the grand emperor, Gotoba, was very sorry about Sanetomo's death. Then the messenger saw Yoshitoki and delivered the overture of the grand emperor, Gotoba, that the heads of two districts in the current Osaka Prefecture should be

---

165) Gomi & Hongō, 10 April, 2010, pp. 72–79.
166) The poem by Sanetomo is in *Kinkai Wakashū* (an old Japanese poetry book) created by him.
167) Ibid. pp. 78–79.
168) By *chōtei*, Masako was given a very high position which was the same as that of Yoritomo, Yoriie, and Sanetomo, which means she was permitted to be the same as a shogun. After Sanetomo died Masako managed the government. She was called an *amashogun* (nun–shogun). Around that time, it was not very often that a nun and a woman were able to receive such a high position.
169) Ibid. p. 82.
170) Ibid. p. 84.

changed.[171] However, Yoshitoki seemed to decline his overture. The shogunate had a right to decide who was the heads of the districts. Masako again sent Hōjō Tokifusa to *chōtei* to discuss the issue of the heir.[172] However, the offer of the shogunate seemed not to be accepted. As a consequence, Fujiwara no Mitora (later Yoritsune) was decided to be the next shogun.[173]

At that time Mitora (Yoritsune) was only in his second year. He was the third son of Fujiwara no Michiie, one of the highest court aristocracies. His mother was also from the highest court noble and a grandchild of Yoritomo's sister. On June 3, 1219, the shogunate received the announcement that he was going to arrive at Kamakura on July 19th. After finishing some events in Kyoto, he arrived with many people and ended up a regent, at Hōjō Yoshitoki's home where a new building was constructed. Since he was still a child, Masako supported him, deciding affairs associated with the shogunate and Yoshitoki moved into action. On December 1, 1220 when Mitora was in his third year, a ceremony of his first wearing of the *hakama* (formal men's divided skirt) was held and Masako assisted him.[174]

Because all of the lineal descendants of Minamoto no Yoritomo passed away, the grand emperor, Gotoba, who had aimed at imperial restoration previously, ordered warriors in twelve districts to kill Hōjō Yoshitoki. On May 15, 1221,[175] a letter talking about putting Yoshitoki to death from *chōtei* arrived at Kamakura. The letter was opened at Masako's residence. There, Miura Yoshimura with a letter from his brother read, "I am ordered to murder Yoshitoki from *chōtei*. After ending him, I would get what I want as a reward." He then visited Yoshitoki. Yoshimura insisted that he did not have such an intention, ignoring the letter of his brother. Fortunetellers were also gathered

171) Gomi & Hongō, 10 April, 2010, p. 85.
172) Ibid. p. 86.
173) Ibid. p. 87.
174) Ibid. p. 98.
175) Jokyū no Ran (the Jokyū War)

there and they augured a good future for the Kamakura Shogunate.[176]

Masako told her subordinate warriors, "Everyone, listen to me as one. This is my last statement. After Yoritomo established Kamakura Shogunate, your lives became much better than before. Benefits given to you are very great, higher than any other mountains and deeper than any other seas. I hope that all of you would like to reciprocate his favors. Now the grand emperor gave us an unreasonable order. If you feel obligated to Yoritomo, defeat the enemy. But if you want to take the side of the grand emperor, say so now. (You can go.)" After having given her speech, all the warriors remembered Yoritomo's favors toward them and grew emotional, deciding to fight the foes.[177]

In the house of Hōjō Yoshitoki a war counsel was held by senior warriors. There were two opinions. One was that after the adversary came to Ashigara and Hakone, the present Kanagawa Prefecture, the shogunate army will fight with them, and the other was that the shogunate army will go to Kyoto to defeat the adversary. Yoshitoki asked Masako's advice. Masako said that he should send the army to Kyoto as soon as possible. Hōjō Tokifusa, Masako's brother, and Hōjō Yasutoki, her nephew left for Kyoto with their army.[178]

An intense fight then developed, and finally the army led by Tokifusa and Yasutoki overcame that of the *chōtei*. On June 15, 1221, the grand emperor, Gotoba sent Yoshitoki a letter saying, "The war was plotted not by me but by my subordinate warriors and some court nobles. I'll accept all of your requests and please make your warriors calm down."[179] The grand emperor,

---

176) Gomi & Hongō, 10 April, 2010, p. 103. The origin of the occasion was Yoshitoki's refusing the grand emperor, Gotoba's offer to dismiss the heads of the two districts. Gotoba's concubine asked him to advise Yoshitoki of the issue. Although the grand emperor, Gotoba ordered Yoshitoki to do so twice, he never obeyed saying, "Because the two heads did not have any faults, we can't take their territories." In the old days people spoke to fortunetellers when they had a problem and accepted their divinations.

177) Ibid. pp. 103–104. Yoritomo made an effort to build the government controlled by the warriors that was independent from *chōtei*. Owing to his effort, the warrior's life changed and became much better. Before, warriors were treated as *chōtei*'s guard dogs and their lives were not good. Because of this, they were very thankful to Yoritomo.

178) Ibid. pp. 104–105.

179) Ibid. p. 120.

38

Gotoba put his guilt on his warriors and court nobles. Some people taking the side of the grand emperor, Gotoba, were killed and some killed themselves. Accommodations of Gotoba's army were set on fire, and people in Kyoto ran away. A lot of injured people and dead men were strewn about the roads. There were neither harmless houses nor rice seedlings in cultivated fields.[180] The fight resulted in many victims.

Handling of the war was conducted by the shogunate. After the war, Hōjō Yasutoki and Hōjō Tokifusa entered Rokuhara[181] in Kyoto, and began to investigate their warriors' exploits. They listed the names of those who killed the enemies, who were injured, and so forth, sending them to Kamakura, and the numbers of the names were numerous. Although the main culprits taking sides with *chōtei* were strictly punished, the punishments toward suspicious people were not severe.[182] For example, after the war the grand emperor, Gotoba became a Buddhist priest[183] and later he was assigned to Oki, the present Shimane Prefecture.[184] The grand emperor, Juntoku, Gotoba's third son, was also sent to Sado, the current Niigata Prefecture.[185] Bōmon Tadanobu, one of the main culprits standing by *chōtei*'s side was not executed because his sister, Sanetomo's legal wife[186] sent Masako a letter to ask for his commutation.[187] Masako divided almost 3,000 territories, taking from traitors and giving to her warriors with great achievements during the war.[188]

The important advantage from the war for the Kamakura Shogunate was the 3,000 territories in western Japan that the government took. It means

180) Gomi & Hongō, 10 April, 2010, p. 120–121.
181) Later, Rokuhara Tandai was established here. It was an agency directly controlled by the shogunate in order to cope with battles (the court), keep safety around Kyoto, and watch *chōtei*. Before the war, the area around Kyoto was managed by the *chōtei*.
182) Gomi & Hongō, 10 April, 2010, p. 121.
183) Ibid. p. 140.
184) Ibid. p. 142.
185) Ibid. p. 143.
186) After Sanetomo's death she entered a nunnery.
187) Gomi & Hongō, 10 April, 2010, p.145.
188) Tabata, 2003, p. 147.

that the shogunate's basic economics very much increased, which helped the shogunate in eastern Japan make its way into western Japan. This was Kamakura Shogunate's nationwide development plan. After Sanetomo's death, the situation of the government was unstable but it was then secured because of the benefit. Although before the war the power of the *chōtei* was stronger than the shogunate, afterwards their powers became more equal and even towards the side of the government.

Hōjō Yoshitoki, Masako's brother, a regent of the Kamakura Shogunate passed away.[189] He helped Yoritomo when he established the Kamakura Shogunate, supported Yoriie as a senior warrior and assisted Sanetomo as a regent. What's more, he always worked as Masako's right hand. On June 12, 1224, his health spiraled downhill. Although fortune-tellers predicted that he would get well soon, he 'crossed the river' owing to beriberi and sunstroke on June 13th. Before breathing his last breath, he became a Buddhist priest. He was in his sixty-second[nd] year and on June 19th a memorial service for his death was held.[190]

On June 28, when Hōjō Yasutoki, Yoshitoki's first son visited Masako's home, she told him to manage the government with Tokifusa, Masako's brother to support the infant, Mitora (later Yoritsune). Yasutoki took over his father's position. Because the situation of the shogunate was unstable after Yoshitoki's death, Masako needed to decide the next regent as soon as possible.[191]

The situation of the shogunate was unstable because dead Yoshitoki's second wife, and her brother, Iga Mitsumune plotted to get rid of Yasutoki and have her real son, Masamura become a regent. In addition, they tried to let Ichijō Sanemasa, the husband of her real daughter take the position of shogun since they wanted to control the shogunate. Iga Mitsumune and Masamura often visited his sister and Miura Yoshimura to talk about the plot secretly. A

---

189) Gomi & Hongō, 10 November, 2010, p. 36.
190) Ibid. pp. 35–37.
191) Ibid. pp. 37–38.

40

servant then got wind of it and relayed it to Yasutoki, however, he ignored it.[192]

After receiving this information, Masako visited Miura Yoshimura on July 17th, 1224. Although Masako asked Yoshimura about the plot, at first, he said that he did not know about it. When Masako again questioned him pretty heavily, finally he told her, "Masamura did not have any issue but Iga Mitsumune and Yoshitoki's second wife seemed to have an evil agenda. I promise I strongly disagreed with them." Then Masako went back to her house.[193] The next day Miura Yoshimura visited Yasutoki saying, "When Yoshitoki was alive, he was very nice to me. I never forgot it. Because both you and Masamura are his sons, I'm not partial to either. I wish only for a safe world. After I severely argued with Iga Mitsumune, he understood me." Yasutoki was neither surprised nor happy. "I have no evil intentions toward Masamura," he said. "I won't fight with him."[194] Later, Masako gathered her senior warriors and said, "The shogun was still too young to deal with subordinate warriors' revolts and it is difficult for me to help him owing to my old age. Everyone, remember the benefits from Yoritomo to all of you and support the little shogun working together." Then after talking about the issue, they recognized that Ichijō Sanemasa, Iga Mitsumune, and Yoshitoki's second wife had an ambitious agenda. Because Ichijō Sanemasa was in a noble court, he was sent to Kyoto to be punished by chōtei. Regarding Iga Mitsumune and Yoshitoki's second wife, they were moved aside.[195]

More than forty years passed after Yoritomo received Mochihitoō's order to hunt down and kill the Heike Family in 1180 and some things changed. For instance, during Yoritomo's time, the warrior mainly focused on fighting and hunting, however, this activity gradually disappeared. Now Hōjō Yasutoki, who is courteous, nice to people, judicious, familiar with the law, respecting of Buddhist affairs, and austere grew up. What's more, Kamakura changed from a

192) Gomi & Hongō, 10 November, 2010, pp. 38–39.
193) Ibid. pp. 40–41.
194) Ibid. p. 41.
195) Ibid. pp. 42–43.

savage military town to a big city being similar to Kyoto.

Hōjō Yasutoki, Yoriie's cousin, is a person who previously told Yoriie's close warrior to advise Yoriie to refrain from entertainments such as *temari* ball because it was a time when people were suffering from famine and extraordinary natural tragedies occurred. Since that time, Yasutoki seemed to be more judicious than Yoriie. Moreover, at Yoshitoki's death, his assets were distributed between his children, and Yasutoki received only a little, saying, "I'm a regent and I won't fight with my brothers because of the assets. It is ok for me to give them to my brothers." Masako felt admiration for his attitude.[196] She must have thought it right that Yasutoki became a regent of the Kamakura Shogunate. In 1232, he established Goseibai Shikimoku (law for warriors), and it was the model of the trial of the government managed by the warrior.

On June 2, 1225, Masako was sick and on the 12th prayer for her recovery was held.[197] On July 11th she departed this life when she was in her sixty-nineth year. Masako's death was told to the public, many people becoming Buddhist priests.[198] Takenogosho,[199] Yoriie's daughter, managed her Buddhist services.[200] In April, 1227 a temple was built[201] for her memorial service which was held in July.[202] After Takenogosho passed away, Yasutoki diligently held her memorial services every year.[203] Masako seemed to be loved and respected by a lot of people during her life and after her death.

---

196) Gomi & Hongō, 10 November, 2010, p. 46.
197) Ibid. pp. 58–59.
198) Ibid. pp. 60–61.
199) She married Yoritsune, the shogun, when she was in her twenty–eighth year. He was in his thirteenth year. However, four years later she died after giving birth.
200) Gomi & Hongō, 10 November, 2010, p. 61.
201) Ibid. p. 96.
202) Ibid. p. 105.
203) Gomi & Hongō, 10 February, 2012, p. 56.

Chapter 2: *Hino Tomiko*

Hino Tomiko was born in 1440 as the daughter of a middle-class noble family in the current Kyoto Prefedture, Japan. She married Ashikaga Yoshimasa, the eighth shogun of the Muromachi Shogunate, on August 27, 1455.The Ashikagas and the Hinos kept up a good relationship with each other since Hino Kenshun, a monk, helped Ashikaga Takauji, the founder of the Ashikaga Shogunate, during a war around the early fourteenth century.[204] The custom of accepting a Hino's daughter as a legal wife to the Ashikaga began when Yoshimitsu (1358 – 1408), the third shogun, tied the knot with Hino Nariko. He loved her very much and the Hino's girls were his favorite. He also

Hino Tomiko

The statue of Hino Tomiko after she became a Buddhist priest. It is owned by Hōkyō-ji, Japan. The image was obtained from Wikipedia in accordance with the Creative Commons license attribution.

---

204) Mitani 1994, pp. 23–24.

44

had Yasuko, Nariko's niece, become his secondary wife. Yoshimitsu chose Eiko, Yasuko's younger sister, as a legal wife to his son, Yoshimochi,[205] the fourth shognate.[206] However, Yoshimochi's son, Yoshikazu, the fifth shogun, rejected the Hino's girls because he didn't like his father, never following his father's advice. After Yoshikazu died in his nineteenth year without having had children, Yoshinori, Yoshimochi's younger brother, became the sixth shogun. Yoshinori followed the precedents and accepted Muneko, Yasuko's niece, as his lawful wife. Shigeko, Yasuko's younger sister, became the secondary wife of Yoshinori, giving birth to the seventh and eighth shoguns. After Yoshinori was killed,[207] Shigeko was very influential to the shogunate, selecting Tomiko, a daughter of her nephew, Hino Masamitsu, as Yoshimasa's wedded wife.[208]

The eighth shogun, Yoshimasa, was only six when his father, Yoshinori, was murdered. His older brother, Yoshikatsu, took over his father's position at the age of eight. However, eight months later, he died of a disease. Because of this, Yoshimasa was formally inaugurated as the eighth shogun in 1449.[209]

When Tomiko married Yoshimasa, he already kept some bedmates, having had three daughters. He was known as a 'lady-killer'. Around that time period, men of the aristocracy usually had many wives owing to a polygamous society.[210] Imamairi was his favorite. She was a warrior's daughter and older than he. Her position was as his nanny. Shigeko, Yoshimasa's mother, was not affectionate with Yoshimasa very much since he was her second son. She gave her first son her deep affection. Due to this reason, he did not love her very

---

205) According to Mitani, Eiko was a secondary wife. (1994, p. 32)
206) In those days, the family was the basic unit in Japan and marriage was not for the sake of the individual, but for families (houses). A man usually had to marry a woman decided by his parents.
207) Yoshinori was nice to Hino's girls. But he suspended Hino Yoshisuke because he interfered with politics. According to the rumor, he might be killed by a person related to Yoshisuke.
208) Izawa September 10, 1999, pp. 96–98.
209) Takano 1978, pp. 106–107.
210) Mitani 1994, pp. 44–45.

much and always trusted Imamairi. Sooner or later, she became his bedmate and also gave birth to his daughter. Gradually, she had also come to fuss about politics, being like his second brain. Shigeko did not like Imamairi and Yoshimasa who always mindlessly followed her.[211]

There were three people who tried to control the politics of that time. They were Karasuma Suketō, Arima Mochiie, and Imamairi, being called "the three devils". Imamairi was the worst. Yoshimasa had neither a firm character for a warrior nor abilities to be a politician. He was a person of refined taste, who only loved culture. Imamairi took advantage of him.[212] Shigeko became very angry at the situation and got rid of Imamairi with a warrior's help. However, Yoshimasa brought her back before long because he loved her very much.[213]

At that point, although Tomiko married into Yoshimasa's family, her severe life began. Yoshimasa did not accept her at first because Imamairi prevented him from approaching her. She eventually made it in to see him and also sent a young girl, Ōdachi Sako, to him to spend a night with him.[214]

The most important thing for women at that time was to give birth to a boy who would become a successor to the Ashikaga Shogunate. First, Sako was carrying a child, but it was a girl. All of Yoshimasa's children were girls. Almost four years after Tomiko married him, she became pregnant by Yoshimasa. She was so happy and she very much wanted to have a boy. In 1459 then, finally, she brought a baby into the world. Yoshimasa earnestly expected this baby and rushed to Tomiko by horse. However, the baby died soon after.[215] Regarding the baby's sex, no one actually knows. Some people say it was a boy and others mention that it was a girl. Anyway, both Tomiko and Yoshimasa were very much disappointed.[216]

211) Mori 1996, pp. 370–371.
212) Dōmon 2004, p. 277.
213) Mori 1996, pp. 370–371.
214) Mori 1996, p. 372.
215) In those days, the mortality rate of babies and infants was very high: 70–80 percent.
216) Mitani 1994, pp. 51–55.

After the baby passed away, a rumor was circulated that the baby had been killed because Imamairi together with Sako had called down a curse upon it. Ōdachi Noriuji, Sako's brother, went to a shrine and asked a monk to pray for the baby to die. Tomiko used the rumor and told it to Yoshimasa. He became very angry and had Imamairi arrested, sending her to Oki Island near Lake Biwa in present Shiga Prefecture.[217] Since at that time, people believed that casting a hex was absolutely effective, it was natural for her to receive some form of punishment. Tomiko, supported by Shigeko and her brother, Hino Katsumitsu,[218] told Yoshimasa that the punishment was not enough. Yoshimasa then decided to give Imamairi a capital offense.[219] Imamairi had trusted Yoshimasa and insisted on her innocence, expecting his help to the end, but it was in vain. Finally, she decided to kill herself by stabbing her breast with a sword. Her life was then short, and was a little more than thirty years.[220] After Imamairi's death, Tomiko began to push her nose into politics as Shigeko and Imamairi had done.[221]

After Imamairi breathed her last, the most bizarre phenomena appeared in Kyoto. In the summer of the year when two suns were in the sky, droughts, catastrophic floods, very cold temperatures, famines, and so forth occurred.[222] Because of a catastrophic flooding of the Kamo River in Kyoto, a lot of people died and an epidemic began. Rice failed its harvest and so its price increased, leaving many dead also from starvation. Peasant uprisings occurred. Bizarre phenomena continued into the next year too. After surviving the drought, they had to weather long rainy days and the rice plants went rotten. To top it all off,

---

217) Because Yoshimasa was so enraged over Imamairi, the dead child might have been a boy.
218) Hino Katsumitsu was Tomiko's elder brother. He took good care of Tomiko and they had a good relationship with each other. After Tomiko married Yoshimasa, Katsumitsu rose to a higher position, also interfering with politics.
219) Mitani 1994, pp. 56–58.
220) Mori 1996, p. 372.
221) Tabata, 1986, p. 90.
222) Mori 1996, p. 373.

due to a plague of locusts, they fed on the crops.[223] People became afraid of the natural disasters, saying that they were Imamairi's haunting. Back in those days, people believed that a person who died as a victim exacted revenge after their death.[224]

What's more, Imamairi's ghost seemed to affect Tomiko, as well. She succumbed to an illness of uncertain origin and was troubled with evil spirits every night. After Tomiko held a service for Imamairi's soul, she then recovered.[225]

Shigeko was also sick in bed. It was natural for her to be the intended recipient of the curse because Shigeko fought with Imamairi all the way. She was also the mother of Yoshimasa who betrayed her, sending her to Oki Island, in the current Shiga Prefecture. Although a famous doctor tried to save her, she was declining rapidly. Finally, the doctor gave up. In spite of Tomiko's holding a service for her, Shigeko crossed the river of death. Tomiko seemed to be very afraid of Imamairi's curse since she held a service for Imamairi again.[226]

When the people were struggling terribly with the natural disasters, what was Yoshimasa doing? He was renovating a palace called Hana no Gosho (mansion with lots of flowers) on Muromachi Street in Kyoto. He set out a gorgeous and stately residence, spending a huge amount of money. He not only requested expensive trees and garden rocks but invited first-class painters to paint wonderful pictures.[227] He also built a brilliant residence for his mother, Shigeko.[228] Furthermore, he enjoyed outer amusements. He sometimes went to Nara Prefecture and so on for junkets with great pageantry, ignoring the people dying of famine on the streets. Moreover, because he loved his imported luxuries, he sent for gorgeous pictures, porcelains, and potteries

---

223) Mitani 1994, p. 79.
224) Mori 1996, p. 373.
225) Ibid.
226) Mitani 1994, pp. 63–64.
227) Izawa June 11, 1999, p. 120.
228) Hatakeyama 1994, p. 76.

from China.[229] Additionally, he often invited over a number of warriors and noblemen, holding banquets with lavish food and drink. They enjoyed singing, dancing, and other festivities.[230] He also hired entertainers, paying a great deal of money.[231]

Who covered the expenses for Yoshimasa's spending? The common people. Yoshimasa gathered plenty of money from people as taxes. He took their rice despite their hunger and imposed hard labor in return.[232] He also received passenger taxes from seven entrances (Shichikō no Seki)[233] in Kyoto, under the pretext that the money would be spent to build Ise Shrine in present Mie Prefecture.[234] Actually, he received most of the money, spending just a little for the shrine.

What did he then do for the dead and people struggling with famine in hard times? He asked monks in a temple in Kyoto to pray for the deceased and donated a little money to the struggling people. He also prepared meals out-of-doors for them. However, his help was too meager to save them. What he did almost didn't work at all.[235] He seemed not to understand people's situation at all in those days as his life was affluent, never experiencing any hardship.

In 1463, Tomiko gave birth to a third child but it was not a boy. Both Tomiko and Yoshimasa were severely disappointed again. Although he allowed himself to enjoy the pleasure of entertainments, he always dwelt on the issue that they didn't have a son, an heir of the shogunate. He had been looking forward to leaving the position of the shogun to take pleasure in the arts with

229) Izawa June 11, 1999, p. 120. Since at that time China was more developed than Japan in almost every aspect of culture, people of high position in Japan were interested in Chinese culture and the rest.
230) Hatakeyama 1994, p. 76.
231) Mitani 1994, p. 89.
232) Izawa 1999 (a), p. 120.
233) Many people on horseback came and went to Kyoto from a lot of places. The shogunate set up seven checking stations and imposed a travelling tax.
234) Mitani 1994, p. 91.
235) Izawa June 11, 1999, p. 120.

his refined tastes. He actually stood up poorly to the position.[236] He didn't like the duties of the shogun, such as attending ceremonies, governing for the betterment of the people, etc. He wanted to give up such duties and find pleasure for himself arbitrarily.[237]

In the course of time, he took up the idea that his younger half-brother, Gijin, a Buddhist monk, could succeed his place after Gijin was re-secularized.[238] Yoshimasa spoke to Gijin about the issue: however, he didn't agree with him. Gijin explained, "Both you and your wife are still young and there are possibilities to have male babies in the future. If you had a boy, I would be nothing." Yoshimasa understood what Gijin was saying because there was no guarantee that Tomiko would never have a baby boy. But Yoshimasa offered, "If we have a boy, I will have him become a Buddhist monk. So then you would not be nothing." Yoshimasa then gave a clear commitment to install Gijin as the next shogun. At last, he agreed with him and Gijin left his temple. After that, he changed his name from Gijin to Yoshimi in December, 1464.[239] Hosokawa Katsumoto became his guardian.[240] Later, Yoshimi accepted Tomiko's younger sister as his wife.[241]

The following year, Tomiko succeeded in getting pregnant again. Not only Katsumitsu, her brother, but all of the Hinos expected a baby boy. Because the boy is the successor of the Ashikaga Shogunate, they would have the authority over politics behind him. Before Tomiko delivered, Yoshimasa's concubine brought a male baby into the world as well. Since Tomiko was pregnant and irritated, she told her inner circle to banish the concubine and the baby. She thought that if her baby was a girl again, the male boy might be the successor in the future. Subsequently, a lady's maid had given birth to a boy. Tomiko again

---

236) Mitani 1994, p. 94.
237) Izawa June 11, 1999, p. 123.
238) The third shogun Yoshimitsu decided that boys who didn't take over the position of the shogun needed to become monks in order to avoid a dispute about the succession.
239) Dōmon 2015, pp. 59–60.
240) Mori 1996, p. 373.
241) Takano 1978, p. 119.

ordered those surrounding her to get rid of her and her baby immediately. One theory holds that Yoshimasa sent the baby to the temple to become a Buddhist monk after considering Tomiko's feelings then. Yoshimi worried that the baby might be male. Finally, after long last, Tomiko birthed a boy. She was so happy and she cried. Yoshimasa rushed to Tomiko on horseback. He was absolutely joyful, too, because the baby was from his wedded wife. The boy was named Yoshihisa.[242]

Yoshimasa then started to have mixed feelings as he had already decided that the next shogun was going to be Yoshimi. Although Yoshimi declined Yoshimasa's offer the first time, he didn't want to give the position to Yoshihisa now. Yoshimi also trusted Yoshimasa. He longed for the palace and its authority, possessing a strong determination to become the next top leader. He didn't like Yoshihisa, not feeling love for him at all, in spite of his being his nephew.[243]

Tomiko was irritated since she earnestly wanted Yoshihisa, her lovely son, to become the next successor. She never allowed Yoshimi to take over Yoshimasa's place. One day Yoshimasa asked Tomiko, "When are we going to send Yoshihisa to a temple?" She answered, "I'll never send him there." She then gave a firm "No" to Yoshimasa. However, in actual fact, she was afraid that Yoshihisa would not be able to become a shogun.[244]

Ise Sadachika,[245] the foster parent, then devised a conspiracy about Yoshimi with the Hinos.[246] Ise Sadachika addressed Yoshimasa, "Yoshimi is planning to kill you because you changed your mind, helping Yoshihisa

---

242) Mitani 1994, pp. 107–110.
243) Dōmon 2015, p. 60.
244) Ibid.
245) Ise Sadachika took in Yoshihisa to foster him. Back in those days, people in high positions did not bring up their children by themselves.
246) Tomiko and her brother, Hino Katsumitsu, might have thought that Yoshihisa's status of the shogun is promised after Yoshimi falls from the position. They seem to aim at controlling the shogunate when young Yoshihisa becomes a top leader. Ise Sadachika loves Yoshihisa very much because he is his nurturing foster parent. He wants Yoshihisa to be the shogun in the future, too. What's more, he also wants to have authority on politics behind Yoshihisa.

succeed your place." They expected that Yoshimasa would accept Yoshihisa as the next shogun: however, at first Yoshimasa did not trust what Ise Sadachika presented.[247] However, he then had second thoughts about the issue because the situation had changed. When Yoshimasa asked anxiously for Yoshimi to take his position, Yoshihisa was not yet born. Yoshimasa now regretted that his decision was premature. Recently he tried to avoid Yoshimi since he doesn't want to talk to him about the matter. Yoshimi likely had a dim view of it. Yoshimasa thought that Yoshimi might end up killing him. On the other hand, Yoshimi was so surprised at this, as he never dreamt of such a thing. First Yoshimi explained the problem to Yamana Sōzen and Hosokawa Katsumoto, who protected Yoshimi. They then visited Yoshimasa and talked about it. Finally, they recognized that the gossip was a lie perpetrated by Ise Sadachika. Soon he ran away, leaving Kyoto for Ōmi, now Shiga Prefecture.[248]

Actually, Yoshimasa must have thought of Yoshihisa as his successor since Yoshihisa is his eldest son, getting sweeter and sweeter by the day. But Yoshimasa felt indebted to Yoshimi, because he had already left the temple, believing their promise that a baby boy would be going into a temple owing to Yoshimasa's firm decision. Yoshimasa wanted to retire early and enjoy life with his entertainments after he left the position despite his young age. Tomiko also insisted that Yoshimasa should not forsake his status. He then decided to relinquish his plan of retiring in his shogunate position because this would mean Yoshimi's success.[249] Yamana Sōzen was then chosen as Yoshihisa's guardian.[250]

247) According to Dōmon (2015, p. 60), when Hosokawa Katsumoto asked Yoshimasa about the gossip, he laughed it off, clearly presenting it was not true.
248) Mitani 1994, pp. 121–125. Later Tomiko called Ise Sadachika back by getting permission from Yoshimasa because Sadachika was an important person for the son, Yoshihisa. Because Sadachika had been Yoshimasa's foster parent, as well, Yoshimasa could not have a severe attitude toward Sadachika. The Ise family was determined to be the Ashikagas' nurturing parent from generation to generation.
249) Izawa June 11, 1999, p. 123.
250) Mori 1996, p. 373.

Yamana Sōzen was father-in-law of Hosokawa Katsumoto. He was a smart, fair man and a great politician, deserving of taking over the Ashikaga Shogunate himself. As Katsumoto followed his own wisdom, he didn't follow his father-in-law very easily. Actually, Katsumoto's status was higher than that of Sōzen.[251] Regarding their personal characters, the younger Katsumoto was rather conservative while the older Sōzen was liberal. Sōzen was familiar with the noble men who were extremely backward; just following old customs and precedents. However, Sōzen sometimes ignored the old habits and received complaints from them. On the other hand, Katsumoto thought much of order and peace. Because of their differences, they were opposed to each other about politics,[252] yet both of them had large reins of power in the shogunate, dividing its power into two parts. It was only a matter of time that their relationship was going to blow up.[253] A lot of power struggles and disputes about the succession of the families occurred around that time.

The Ōnin War (1467 – 1477) broke out because wrangling about the successions of the Shibas and the Hatakeyamas[254] developed into a power struggle between Katsumoto and Sōzen, including a fight about taking over the place of Yoshimasa. The head of the Eastern army was Hosokawa Katsumoto and that of the West was Yamana Sōzen. The war continued for eleven years, mainly in Kyoto.

Regarding the Shiba family, after Shiba Yoshitake, a young family head passed away in his eighteenth year, leaving them without a successor in the family. Then Yoshitoshi from a branch house took over the status of the head.

---

251) Katsumoto's position was followed by that of the shogun, the highest position of a subordinate warrior, while Sōzen's status was following Katsumoto's. However, when Ashikaga Yoshinori, the sixth shogun, was murdered, Sōzen very much contributed to the issue and finally killed the murderer. After that, the power balance between the two became almost the same.
252) Dōmon 2015, p. 61.
253) Katsumoto adopted Toyohisa, the youngest boy of Sōzen, as his successor. However, later Katsumoto had a birth son and sent Toyohisa to a temple to become a monk. After that, their relationship worsened.
254) The rank of the Shibas and the Hatakeyamas was the same as that of the Hosokawas.

However, he had strong sentiments and sometimes had trouble with Yoshimasa. Once, Hosokawa Katsumoto helped him so that Yoshitoshi could reaffirm a good relationship with Yoshimasa. Because of Yoshitoshi's character, there was a person who insisted that Yoshikado, a son of the Shiba family in Kyūshū, receive the head of the position. In light of this background, Yamana Sōzen, being against Katsumoto, seemed to recommend the person to do so.[255]

In addition, the Hatakeyamas were also struggling over the succession of the family. Since Hatakeyama Mochikuni did not have his own son, Masanaga, his younger brother's son, was adopted as his successor. However, later a baby boy, Yoshinari, was born between Mochikuni and his concubine. This is the same case as that of Tomiko and Yoshimasa. After the baby was birthed, Mochikuni changed his mind, deciding to give his position to his own son, Yoshinari. Hosokawa Katsumoto helped Masanaga on the other hand, and Yoshinari depended on Yamana Sōzen. There were two headmen in the Hatakeyama family, too. Masanaga's party and Yoshinari's repeated a bitter fight. After the battles continued for almost six years, Masanaga, supported by Yoshimasa, defeated Yoshinari, and Yoshinari was exiled from the capital by the shogunate.[256]

Yamana Sōzen asked Tomiko to help Yoshinari so that he would create a good relationship with Yoshimasa, and proceed to the capital. Because Yamana Sōzen was Yoshihisa's guardian, she needed his aid in order to make Yoshihisa the next shogun. She accepted his request and talked to Yoshimasa. With regard to Yoshimasa, he didn't like Yoshinari as the shogunate, suffering from the six-year battles. Although he might be a reliable warrior for Sōzen, Yoshimasa was also afraid of him, not making him feel welcome. However, Tomiko persuaded him to accept Yoshinari. Tomiko seemed to have a stronger feeling for politics from the standpoint that Yoshimasa followed her opinion.[257]

---

255) Mitani 1994, pp. 114–116.
256) Mitani 1994, pp. 116–118, 126.
257) In the Muromachi Era, the shogun interfered with the succession of the families. The families needed to receive permission of the shogun for who would become their next headman.

After Yoshinari was accepted by Yoshimasa, Yoshinari invited him and other important warriors to dinner at Sōzen's house. Then Yoshinari advanced his ideas on Yoshimasa as he wanted to regain the residence where Masanaga lived. Yoshimasa agreed with him and ordered Masanaga to leave the house, which meant an ouster. In actuality, Sōzen pulled strings behind the scenes as a puppet master. On this occasion he wanted to make the status of Hosokawa Katsumoto supporting Masanaga weaker by helping Yoshinari. Masanaga reacted to the betrayal with explosive anger, raising an army but in vain. He eloped instead.[258]

Hosokawa Katsumoto, taking Masanaga's side, gathered troops secretly. First, he pummeled a family related to the Yamanas, protecting Yoshimasa after occupying the shogunate. The Hosokawa family, Hatakeyama Masanaga, Shiba Yoshitoshi, and others were the East squad while the Yamana family, Hatakeyama Yoshinari, Shiba Yoshikado, and the rest were the West one.[259]

Hosokawa Katsumoto then won Ashikaga Yoshimasa to his side and kept the emperor and grand emperor in his own custody.[260] Katsumoto called on his government forces and rebel army. He built up 160,000 warriors from twenty-four areas, while on the other hand, Yamana Sōzen gathered 90,000 from twenty regions.[261]

In regards to Ashikaga Yoshimi, he fled down to the existing Ise, the current Mie Prefecture. Tomiko said to Yoshimasa, "Yoshimi left Kyoto for Ise. It is clear that he has no intention of taking over your position. You should now

---

258) Mitani, 1994 pp. 126–132; 136–137.
259) Mitani, 1994 pp. 137–139.
260) Tomiko very much opposed Hosokawa Katsumoto's demand that Yoshimasa stand by his side and tried to persuade Yoshimasa not to accept it. Katsumoto needed Yoshimasa's help since he wanted people to think of his army as an imperial force. Because Yamana Sōzen's power became weaker, it would be difficult for Yoshihisa to take over the position of the next shogun. However, Yoshimasa did not agree with Tomiko. Yoshimasa used to prefer Sōzen but now had a change of heart. As Katsumoto's power was getting stronger, Yoshimasa might be afraid of him. He was a soft man and could not say "no" when someone told him something strongly. Tomiko did not like his flaccidness and her interference with politics was serious business for Yoshimasa.
261) Dōmon 2017, p. 58.

permit Yoshihisa to be your next successor as soon as possible." It is likely that Hino Katsumitsu and Ise Sadachika also promoted her. Because Katsumoto, Yoshimi's guardian, did not agree with Tomiko, he often asked Yoshimi to come back. After Yoshimi returned, he told Yoshimasa to get rid of Katsumitsu and Sadachika in order to help secure his future position. He continued to insist on it. His stubborn attitude irritated Yoshimasa but he felt inclined to get along with him. Observing this situation, Katsumoto decided to abandon Yoshimi, recommending that he become a monk again. Katsumoto wanted to remain in good stead with Yoshimasa. Although Yoshimi was dissatisfied with what Katsumoto said, he moved to Mt. Hiei. He expected Yoshimasa and Katsumoto to take him back soon, but they did not do that.[262] During the war, betraying and being betrayed often occurred.

Sōzen was angry that his party was called a rebel army and chose Ashikaga Yoshimi as their general, declaring that he would become the next shogun. Because the number of Sōzen's warriors was less than that of Katsumoto's, he got together an additional 22,000 troops to solidify his strength.[263] Soon, Katsumoto requisitioned many *ashigaru* (common foot soldiers)[264] because keeping many soldiers was important for his party to pick up a win.[265] Although they continued fierce fighting with each other, the game was not over.

At last, in 1469, Yoshimasa allowed Yoshihisa in his fifth year to turn over his place in a ceremonial way when Yoshimi became general of the enemy. Hosokawa Katsumoto swiftly approached Tomiko and began helping Yoshihisa. She was as happy as his mother. In 1473, Yoshihisa, in his ninth year, was appointed to be the shogun. When the shogun was in his infancy, a foster parent, in this case Ise Sadachika, usually gave aid to him. However, without

---

262) Mitani 1994, pp. 150–152.
263) Dōmon 2017, p. 58.
264) *Ashigaru* didn't consist of regular soldiers but citizen's militia. They attacked their enemy in a group without bearing many arms. In those days they were guerilla–like without discipline or ethics, sometimes committing theft and arson. They drank and created a ruckus in a great number of places. However, later on they became a vital presence in wars.
265) Mitani 1994, p. 149.

56

accepting Sadachika, she decided that she would back Yoshihisa up. Tomiko's power then became stronger thanks to his assuming the post of the shogun.[266]

The capital, Kyoto, was reduced to desolate scenes. Many temples, including that of Ashikaga's Family, shrines, residents of court noblemen, and so forth were burned, some court residents moving Nara Prefecture for safety.[267] Peasant uprisings often occurred,[268] especially for beseeching those of the upper echelon to help poor peasants repudiate moneylender's debt. The system was that they order moneylenders to relinquish getting the money back by returning the promises given to the peasants. People suffered from this levy because of the shogunate's lack of money from the war, in addition to off-and-on flood disasters and famines. People losing their houses and goods had to fight in severe situations.[269] Suffice it to say, there were plenty of dead people on the streets of Kyoto.[270]

What was Yoshimasa doing during a war that was damaging the capital, Kyoto? As usual, he organized a big party with plenty of rich food and drink with many women. One of them suggested, "Let's run away from here because the outside war is terrible." However, Yoshimasa, stayed and drank, saying, "Don't lose your cool. It's not a big problem."[271] Although in fact, Yoshimasa sometimes did everything within his power to avert a war, he was not able to make it happen this time. He was nowhere near the third shogun, with Yoshimitsu's political ability and Tomiko's desire for power, despite very much contributing to develop culture in the Muromachi Era.

How about Tomiko? What was she doing then? As Yoshimasa was not interested in politics and drinking every day, and Yoshihisa being too young to manage the government, Tomiko intervened in politics.[272] She made a strong

---

266) Mitani 1994, pp. 153–154, 162–163.
267) Dōmon 2017, p. 59.
268) Torigoe 2000, pp. 107–108.
269) Dōmon 2017, p. 59.
270) Hatakeyama 1994, p. 79.
271) Dōmon 2017, p. 59.
272) Tabata 1986, p. 91.

effort to multiply her wealth. She thought *daimyō* (feudal lords) in Kyoto that lacked a fortune would need money after the outbreak of the war. Because of this, she began to add to her fortune before the war. She was going to lend them some money.[273] Her financial sense was influenced by her brother, Hino Katsumitsu, who was one of the best moneymakers in that region. Since childhood she learned financial acuity from him.[274] Because the feudal tenure place in Kyoto of the Hino family was a busy commercial area, he was familiar with rich merchants and studied finance.[275] Katsumitsu introduced warriors and people from the aristocracy who wanted to take out a loan to her, getting referral fees from her.[276]

Before the outbreak of the war, Tomiko started to lend money to warriors and court nobles with a high finance charge. When the war was on the verge of breaking out, Yamana Sōzen also visited her in order to borrow some money. At that time her financial business was almost mainstream. She understood what he said and loaned him money, making extra sure of a repayment deadline and receiving a promise to pay from him. During the war after Yoshimi, supported by Sōzen, became a general in the West squad, Tomiko belonged to the East one with Yoshimasa and Yoshihisa. However, she put up money for people in both the East and West squads. This means that she advanced money to her enemies, too, as a war profiteer.[277] Both sides had to spend huge amounts of money for many years. For example, they needed to hire *ashigaru*. If they hired 1000 of them a month, they had to spend 108 million yen. Furthermore, they needed to cover expenses for staying in Kyoto: food, carrying war weapons, and so forth. Because the war continued for eleven years, their expenditures were very heavy.[278]

---

273) Dōmon 2004, p. 280.
274) Takano 1978, p. 124.
275) Azusawa 2018, p. 76.
276) Dōmon 2016, p. 61.
277) Dōmon 2017, p. 59.
278) Mitani 1994, p. 176.

Tomiko's general reputation was not good. Some people pointed out, "She controls the world and makes enormous fortunes by lending a huge amount of money to even her enemies. Morality is confused in Kyoto." However, she remained unconcerned.[279] Others exclaimed, "If she really loved her son, Yoshihisa, she would not lend money to her foes. If they win the war with the money from her, Yoshihisa won't be able to become the shogun. She just promotes the war."[280]

In the Muromachi Era, people already recognized the power of money and Japan evolved into a money economy.[281] They used money rather than rice for the nation's business and land transactions.[282] They respected those with lots of money, calling them the 'lucky wealthy', although they had been looked down on in the old days. The rich contributed to the development of business as those from a newly emerging class. They were called persons of virtue. This was a new value among commoners which was very different from that of warriors, who focused on the class system and military power.[283] At that time, financial institutions such as pawn shops and liquor stores[284] conducted banking matters related to deposits and affairs involving brokerage houses. They established subsidiaries which loaned money to common people, low-class warriors, noblemen, and others, supporting private mutual aid organizations dealing with accommodations. It was the dawn of capitalism in the middle- ages. Instead of warriors, real business, transacted by private institutions, led society.[285]

Tomiko also collected a great deal of taxes from pawn shops and liquor outlets. In the Muromachi Era, there were 350 pawn shops in Kyoto, 200 in

---

279) Dōmon 2017, p. 59.
280) Izawa September 10, 1999, p. 99.
281) Although money was created and introduced in the Nara Era (710 – 794), it took time to be mainstream.
282) In the old days people traded not in money, but in rice.
283) Azusawa 2018, p. 75.
284) Because in those times, liquor shops usually had lots of money, they ran financial businesses, too.
285) Hataketama 1994, p. 75.

Nara, and thirty in Ōmi, Shiga Prefecture. Before the war, they paid almost 240 million yen in taxes. Regarding liquor shops, a shop in Kyoto did seventy-two million yen. She loaned money, collecting interest as merchants did. She already knew that interest accrued and an original principal swelled, so she conducted the system as current banks do. Because she advanced feudal lords and others money, their borrowed sums during the course of the war would be huge. The war, then, allowed her to generate prodigious wealth.[286]

Next, she got a move on the speculative buying of rice by taking advantage of interest from pawn shops and liquor stores.[287] She bought up rice when its price was low and tried to sell it at high cost during lean harvests. People became afraid of her, saying, "She's built storehouses for rice"[288] because at that time, no one in the ruling classes were involved in the market price of rice. Even men.

In addition, Tomiko managed the money from passenger taxes of seven entrances in Kyoto, as well as taxes for houses and rice fields. The taxes for the latter were imposed on people for a temporary period of time when the government needed funds to build temples, shrines, etc. They were important income sources for the shogunate.[289] She then became a loan shark and amassed a personal fortune by utilizing the public domain.[290]

In 1469, the war continued. A major battle involving several regions and betrayers popped up one after another. It was gradually too difficult for both generals, Hosokawa Katsumoto and Yamana Sōzen, to control the war. Sōzen was almost seventy, ill, and war weary. In 1472, he began a peace negotiation with Katsumoto but it was not successful. Although he tried to kill himself with *hara-kiri*, his subordinate warriors saved him. However, he passed away in his seventieth year due to this attempt. Concerning Katsumoto, he was very

---

286) Mitani 1994, pp. 174–175.
287) Hatakeyama 1994, p. 79.
288) Azusawa 2018, p. 76.
289) Ibid.
290) Tabata 1986, pp. 92–93.

shocked about this death and considered becoming a Buddhist monk. After a short time he also passed away due to a cold epidemic. It was his forty-fourth year. The war continued from force of habit and it was about time to end it. Plentiful *daimyō* (feudal lords) withdrew from Kyoto to their domains. This eleven-year war finally ended without a clear result of which side won.[291]

Yoshimasa might not have been very concerned in when and how the war ended as he was instead planning the building of a gorgeous palace for his mountain villa in Higashiyama, Kyoto. He talked to Tomiko about it, asking for her financial support. After Tomiko realized the huge amount of money that would be needed, she declined, saying, "I'm not THAT rich."[292] Actually, donations from *daimyō*, taxes, and so on, were gathered for its expenses. Yoshimasa started the construction in 1482.[293] The third shogun, Yoshimitsu, had also established a lavish palace where the walls were decorated with gold[294] in the west of Kyoto. Following him, Yoshimasa set up a similar one[295] using silver, but it was even more pompous than Yoshimitsu's. There were Buddhist sanctums, his residence, a tearoom, and an expansive garden at his palatial home. His residence was built in Japanese style and the Buddhist sanctums were after the fashion of China. Regarding the tearoom, it was a holy sanctuary with the atmosphere of Zen Buddhism that he was longing for. The garden was designed by the famous gardener Zenami, and covered with moss.[296] The harmony there among a pond, stones, and trees was beautiful, quiet, simple, and elegant. Thanks to this spending largesse, he left a great cultural heritage for his legacy in Japan. He very much contributed to the development of the arts at that time. The culture of the era is now called Higashiyama Bunka. Although he was an ineffective shogun, he was an excellent patron of culture.

---

291) Mitani 1994, pp. 158–160.
292) Dōmon 2016, pp. 59–60.
293) Mitani 1994, p. 187.
294) After Yoshimitsu's death, it became a Zen temple called The Golden Temple. Its official name is Kitayama Rokuon-ji in Japanese.
295) It is called The Silver Temple and its official name is Jishō-ji.
296) Dōmon 2016, p. 60.

After the Ōnin War, Ashikaga Yoshihisa grew to adulthood, becoming a great young shogun. There was a mindset of the day that it was ok for people of low position to contradict traditional authority and values, and push out those of high position, taking their authority by force.[297]

Rokkaku Takayori from Ōmi, the current Shiga Prefecture, grabbed temple and aristocracy's lands. Yoshihisa ordered Takayori to return them to their owners. However, Takayori ignored Yoshihisa's command and Yoshihisa decided to fight him for them.[298] Yoshihisa won every battle. He destroyed Takayori's main castle in current Shiga Prefecture and another where Takayori ran to. He sought refuge in a mountain with his trusted vassals, losing his authority and fortune. In fact, Yoshihisa's victory definitely became final and binding in this situation. At this point, he should have returned to Kyoto and dispersed his forces.[299]

Yoshihisa instead wanted to kill Takayori, following the principle that one should eliminate an enemy when able to do so. The war then continued for a long time and Yoshihisa and his troops remained guarding their territory in the battlefield. Hosokawa Masamoto, a son of Katsumoto, suggested that he withdraw his troops from the place, being Shiga Prefecture. However, he paid no attention to Masamoto at all. Then Masamoto went back to Kyoto. This intractable war needed ongoing resources for its digging in, food, daily necessities, and all that. Because the situation for warriors of low station was not good, dissatisfaction with Yoshihisa increased, but he remained unconcerned, spending lots of money on his entertainments.[300]

The long war was then a death blow for Yoshihisa. Basically, his health was fragile. Before the battle even began, he had been sick, and had fallen into a serious condition. On the battlefield, he again fell ill because of his excessive lifestyle. During the war, he changed his name from Yoshihisa to Yoshihiro, in

---

297) Mitani 1994, p. 196. This mindset is called, "gekokujō".
298) Mitani 1994, pp. 196–197.
299) Izawa September 24, 1999, p. 97.
300) Izawa September 24, 1999, p. 98.

hopes of recovery and victory. However, his situation was not improved and the fight was not yet settled.[301]

Yoshimasa often visited temples to pray for his son's rapid recovery even though he was also sick and elderly at the time. Though he was not fit for managing his political sphere, he was a good, loving father.[302] He sometimes went to see Yoshihiro on the battlefield, sending him a poem in order to cheer him up. He gave his whole talents to the poem, saying that he wished for Yoshihisa's (Yoshihiro's) victory and fast recovery.[303]

Not only Yoshimasa but Tomiko too came straight to Yoshihiro after getting the news that he was very sick. He so grew gaunt and it seemed to be so serious. At that time she advised him on the battle, as inaccurate intel about it might be spread. Later, she again came to see him when he fell into critical condition. Without sleeping, she took care of him by praying and wishing for a miracle. She was then not a person of influence in the shogunate, but just a mother loving her son. Unfortunately, he crossed the river of death in his twenty-fifth year in 1489.[304] When she returned home to Kyoto, she wailed hysterically without ceasing.[305] She managed his funeral, spending about one hundred million yen. Normally, Yoshimasa would be the one does it, however he had already departed his life before the funeral.[306] After his death, she entered a nunnery.[307]

Tomiko had controlled the shogunate anew. She enjoyed a lot more power because she had been the wife of a former shogun and the mother of a present one. But after both Yoshimasa and Yoshihiro passed away, her public influence seemed to fall into a decline. However, such a thing never actually happened.[308]

301) Mitani 1994, pp. 198–200.
302) Izawa September 24, 1999, p. 99.
303) Mitani 1994, p. 199.
304) Mitani 1994, pp. 200–201.
305) Tabata 1986, p. 94.
306) Mitani 1994, p. 203.
307) Tabata 1986, p. 94.
308) Izawa September 24, 1999, p. 99.

She needed to decide the next shogun because Yoshihiro did not have an heir. At first, she recommended Yoshiki, a son between Yoshimi and her sister, as the successor.[309] Although some static did ensue, and there were some troubles, Yoshiki did in fact become the next shogun. However, his father, Yoshimi, interfered with the politics. He tried to push Tomiko away because he blamed her for not winning the position of shogun in the first place, owing to Yoshihiro, her son. Yoshiki also worked to ignore and work against her. She then worked with Hosokawa Masamoto who was not willing to accept Yoshiki, so that they dispatched him by a coup. Masamoto suggested that the next shogun be Seikō, a monk, and Yoshimasa's nephew after Yoshiki's downfall. Seikō then returned to secular life and they helped him accept the place of the shogun. Later on, Seikō changed his name to Yoshitō, Yoshitake, and Yoshizumi. Finally, the eleventh shogun, Ashikaga Yoshimizu became realized.[310] She then adopted him, to have some say in public as his mother and guardian. She was then happy but he seemed not to like his adopted mother.

When Tomiko was in her fifty-fifth year, she became weary due to old age. She neither insisted on her opinions nor gave strong influences to the shogunate. She often visited the emperor's court with some gifts. In 1496, she and the emperor, Gotsuchimikado,[311] enjoyed a ball game together, drinking and chatting. They had a close relationship. After three months her health failed, and she lost consciousness. The emperor paid a courtesy call to her but her coma state persisted. He was worried and at times panicked over this. Finally, she gasped her last. It was in her fifty-seventh year. Although in good time her funeral was held, Yoshizumi did not take part in it. However, as a result, the enormous fortune that she had gathered from the world rolled over to him.[312]

---

309) Tomiko chose Yoshiki, her nephew, who had a blood relationship with the Hino family, probably in order to keep its authority toward the shogunate.
310) Tabata 1986, pp. 94–95.
311) There was a rumor that the relationship between Tomiko and the emperor was adulterous when Yoshimasa was still alive. Some people said Tomiko and Yoshimasa lived separately for a while due to this reason. But no one knew the truth.
312) Mitani 1994, pp. 228–230.

65

Chapter 3: *Yodo-dono*

Yodo-dono was born in 1569[313] when Japan was a place of civil war and upheaval. She was the eldest daughter of Ichi, a sister of Oda Nobunaga,[314] in a chatelain of Kiyosu Castel in now Aichi Prefecture, and Azai Nagamasa,[315]

Yodo-dono

The picture image is said to be Yodo-dono and owned by Nara Prefectural Museum of Art, Japan. The image was obtained from Wikipedia in accordance with the Creative Commons license attribution.

---

313) Some say it was in 1568 and others describe it in 1567. Regarding the age, date, etc., they are sometimes unclear because exact sources were not found.
314) Other views are that Ichi was a daughter of Nobunaga's cousin (Fukuda, 2007, p. 27) or was Nobunaga's cousin,
315) Some people say "Asai".

a castellan of Odani Castel in the current Shiga Prefecture.[316] Yodo-dono was a young lady of fine breeding. When she was a child, she was called Chacha. She had two sisters, Hatsu and Gō, and two brothers, Manpukumaru and Mankikumaru.[317] It is certain that Ichi was the biological mother of the three daughters, but a mother of one of the two sons is not clear. Someone said that his mother was her Nagamasa's secondary wife.[318]

During the civil wars, Oda Nobunaga (1534 – 1582), Chacha's uncle on her mother's side, was the first great *daimyō* (a feudal lord) who led to dominate the whole country in Japan. After the Ōnin War (1467 – 1477), there was a mindset of the day that it was ok for people of low position to contradict traditional authority and values, and push out those of high position, taking their authority by force. Then the Age of Civil Wars began in Japan. Oda Nobunaga was born in 1534 in Owari, the existing Aichi Prefecture, and was known as a rather dense and eccentric fellow when he was young. However, he unified Owari at the age of twenty-five after defeating his enemies, including his brothers and uncle. Before long he came to be known as a strong warrior with fantastic skills for war.[319]

Oda Nobunaga gradually showed his abilities. First, because the noble, powerful Imagawa family tried to take Nobunaga's territory, the Oda squad with around 2,000 warriors and the Imagawa squad with more than 20,000 fought intensely in Okehazama, now Aichi Prefecture in 1560, called Okehazama no Tatakai (the Battle of Okehazama). Although the number of warriors in the Oda squad was much smaller than that of Imagawa's, the Oda squad defeated the Imagawa with a surprise attack. Soon Nobunaga created an alliance with Matsudaira Motoyasu (later, Tokugawa Ieyasu), who was taken hostage by the Imagawa family. After that, Oda Nobunaga started to dominate the other

---

316) Kuwata, 1958, p. 1.
317) A source presents his name as Manjumaru. (Fukuda, 2007, p. 35)
318) Yoshida, 1996, p. 193. There is another view that the first son's biological mother was Ichi, but that of the second son was Nagamasa's concubine. (Fukuda, 2007, p. 35)
319) Ōishi, 2020, pp. 68–69.

areas in order to enlarge his territory. In the course of time, in Kyoto, capital of Japan at that time, the thirteenth shogun, Ashikaga Yoshiteru, was killed and his brother Yoshiaki, returning to secular life asked *daimyōs* to help him become the next shogun. Oda Nobunaga decided to assist him because Nobunaga could rise to an important authority and advocate for the general after his success. He one by one knocked down nuisances disturbing Yoshiaki from achieving the position of the shogun. In the middle of this, he sent his sister Ichi as a legal wife to Azai Nagamasa so as to ally with him because Nobunaga needed the Azai's help in order to assist Yoshiaki.

Finally, Ashikaga Yoshiaki became a shogun, and Nobunaga developed rulers governing the areas around Kyoto to follow Yoshiaki and gradually raise his dominance with economic power. Unfortunately, the relationship between Yoshiaki and Nobunaga was soon growing worse with their struggle for power. Nobunaga attacked Asakura Yoshikage taking the side of Ashikaga Yoshiaki when Yoshiaki had not yet achieved shogun status. Due to the betray of Azai Nagamasa, thinking much of the Asakura family, Nobunaga had a hard fight but finally rode to victory. Ashikaga Yoshiaki came to form anti-Nobunaga power, not only with the Asakuras, the Azais, and Takeda Shingen who was a famous *daimyō* in Kai, the existing Yamanashi Prefecture, but also with Buddhist monks who had a large amount of authority in those days in Japan. Suddenly monks and temple protestors accused Nobunaga to the outbreak of war. For example, in 1571 he destroyed Hieizan Enryaku-ji, the head temple of a Buddhist Tendai sect in now Shiga Prefecture by setting a fire. In addition to the temple, the houses of monks and worshippers also suffered a lot of damage and many people were killed. The war between Nobunaga and the temple culture continued for almost ten years but at last Nobunaga won out. In 1573, Takeda Shingen passed away because of disease, although people associated with anti-Nobunaga power very much expected him to defeat Nobunaga. The plan made by anti-Nobunaga power was in vain. After Shingen's death, Nobunaga attacked the residence of Ashikaga Yoshiaki by setting it on fire, and

Yoshiaki shut him up in a castle in Kyoto, however, finally Yoshiaki was forced to give up, being ousted from Kyoto. This meant the Muromachi Shogunate continuing for 237 years vanished from Kyoto with Ashikaga Yoshiaki.[320]

Oda Nobunaga was also a person of culture who pursued cutting-edge art. His favorite was *chanoyu* (the tea ceremony), that included the arts of gracious etiquette and was one of the general educations that war-torn military commanders needed to learn. He was an expert in this since childhood. In the place of *chanoyu* people built strong relationships, exchanging up-to-date information about the country and talking about politics. He created the license of holding *chanoyu* and only gave it to his subordinate warriors that he trusted, with their social positions being approved by Nobunaga. He loved *sumō* (Japanese-style wrestling), hunting, and dance as well as *chanoyu*. Because he liked new and loud things, his castle was decorated with gold and priceless artwork. He was a fashion leader as well but was most attracted by the new weapon, guns.[321]

The unification of the whole country was near at hand for Oda Nobunaga without worry from most of his enemies, but then it suddenly escaped him due to Akechi Mitsuhide, his subordinate warrior's betrayal. It is still not clear the reason why Akechi Mitsuhide betrayed Nobunaga although there are various opinions. Akechi Mitsuhide respected Nobunaga, being very loyal to him, and Nobunaga very much trusted Mitsuhide, giving him a high position. However, on June 2, 1582 in Honnō-ji, a temple where Nobunaga stayed with his nearly one hundred warriors, it was attacked by Mitsuhide's army with more than 13,000 warriors.[322] Although Nobunaga's warriors tried to protect Nobunaga, they were defeated one by one, flames from guns soon turning around and Nobunaga committed *hara-kiri* in the fire to finish his forty-nine-year life.[323] Later, Nobunaga's administration became the basis of the Toyotomi

---

320) Ōishi, 2020, pp. 69–75, pp. 81–83, pp. 87–93, pp. 96–98.
321) Ōishi, 2020, pp. 98–101.
322) Honnō-ji no Hen (the Honnō-ji Incident).
323) Ōishi 2020, pp. 110–116.

Administration by Toyotomi Hideyoshi, who killed Akechi Mitsuhide soon after Nobunaga's death together with The Edo Shogunate by Tokugawa Ieyasu.

Azai Nagamasa, Chacha's father, was a *daimyō* in the northern part of Ōmi, the existing Shiga Prefecture in Japan. Sukemasa, his grandfather, Hisamasa, his father, and Nagamasa were well known as the Azai three generations. When Sukemasa took over the reign of the family, Kyōgoku Takakiyo ruled there. However, he was not interested in politics and his subordinate senior warrior, Kōsaka Ienobu, actually controlled the Takakiyo, treating other warriors including Sukemasa arrogantly and coercively. Even though after Ienobu's death his son, Nobumitsu, succeeded his place, he was also arrogant and coercive. The warriors, including Sukemasa, then grew sour on Nobumitsu, finally deciding to fight with him. The result ended in their victory.

After that a split among friends happened. Sukemasa was deemed the judge, as he was the leader. Although Sukemasa built a castle in Odaniyama, the current Shiga Prefecture, demonstrating his power to the people, he passed away in 1542. After Sukemasa's death, Hisamatsu took over his position. He tried to open up the way to becoming a war-torn country *daimyō* by mediating disputes that was difficult for many people in his area, this despite a lack of military exploits.[324] Nagamasa was then born in 1545. In 1552, Rokkaku Yoshikata began to attack the Azai family. The Rokkaku family and the Kyōgokus were from the same tribe and the Rokkakus did not accept the Azais as a regent of the Kyōgokus from past times. After a few wars between the two they concluded with reconciliation, but it meant the Azai Hisamasa squad was defeated. Because of this, Nagamasa had to receive the name of Katamasa, which had a part of Yoshikata, when Nagamasa had the ceremony of manhood. It implied that the relationship between the two was not an alliance, but that of sovereign (the Rokkakus) and subordinate warrior (the Azais), which was very humiliating for the Azai family. Moreover, Rokkaku Yoshikata decided

324) Owada 1997, p. 7, pp.10–13.

that Nagamasa's wife, who was a daughter of Yoshikata's subordinate senior warrior, meant that Nagamasa was treated as Yoshitaka's subordinate warrior. However, the Azai family still ruled the north of Ōmi. When Nagamasa was in his sixteenth year, he had his father retire and decided to break off from the Rokkaku family with his subordinate warriors' help, so as to get rid of the pressure from the Rokkakus. There was then an intense war between the Azai squad and the Rokkaku squad, which was called Norada no Tatakai (the Battle of Norada) in 1560. Although the number of the Azai warriors was much smaller than that of the Rokkaku, the Azai squad miraculously won. After that, Nagamasa divorced his wife and changed his name from Katamasa to Nagamasa. He gradually became a great warrior.[325]

A little before Azai Nagamasa had his father retire and took over his position, Oda Nobunaga also succeeded his father's place after his death. Both of them miraculously gained victories in spite of the disadvantageous situations: Nagamasa defeated the Rokkaku squad at the Battle of Norada, in 1560, and Nobunaga triumphed at the Battle of Okehazama, in 1560. They began to distinguish themselves as leaders in the same period and later they met each other.

Regarding Chacha's mother, Ichi, she was a very pretty and obedient woman. People said that she was the most beautiful lady during the Age of the Civil Wars. She had a slender face, long and narrow eyes and a small mouth.[326] Her personality seemed to be amenable and passive to accept her destiny of a political marriage. Following the order of Nobunaga, her brother, first she got married to Azai Nagamasa so as to keep a good alliance between the Oda family and the Azai family.[327] As described above, before marrying Ichi, Nagamasa already had a wife but he divorced her within three months.[328]

Several years later the alliance between the Oda family and the Azai

---

325) Owada, 2008, pp. 10–15.
326) Yoshida, 1996, p. 192.
327) Kuwata, 1958, p. 6.
328) Yoshida, 1996, p. 193.

family was broken because Oda Nobunaga decided to attack the Asakura family that had a deep relationship with the Azai family. Before marriage between Ichi and Nagamasa, Oda Nobunaga promised Azai Nagamasa that the Odas would not attack the Asakuras. However, Oda Nobunaga did not keep his promise and Nagamasa betrayed Nobunaga, helping the Asakura family. Finally, Oda Nobunaga attacked Odani Castle and Azai Nagamasa died there. Although the oldest son of ten years, Manpukumaru, was killed by Hashiba Hideyoshi (later, Toyotomi Hideyoshi), following the order of his master, Nobunaga, Ichi and the three daughters were rescued and sent back to Oda Nobunaga, living in the home of Nobunaga's brother.[329]

After Nobunaga's death, because of a recommendation of the third son of Nobunaga, Ichi with the three daughters married Shibata Katsuie who was a strong, brave senior warrior of Nobunaga as well as a good politician, although Hideyoshi also proposed to Ichi.[330] First Ichi refused to marry again but she finally accepted it. She needed someone to back up her daughters' future after she lost her powerful brother, Nobunaga. Katsuite was the most appropriate person.[331] Shibata Katsuie, having more than ten concubines, was already in his fifties but she was in the middle of her thirties. Ichi, Nobunaga's sister was a special woman for Katsuie, and he very much cherished her. Their relationship was good and she was happy. However, a power break between Katsuie and Hideyoshi occurred. Katsuie was defeated by Hideyoshi, falling on his sword in his castle. Before Katsuie died, he recommended Ichi to leave the castle with the three daughters in order to keep their heads above water. However, she did not accept his recommendation and died with him, the three daughters being saved.[332] They were sent to Hideyoshi's armed camp.[333] Ichi might have been an unhappy but beautiful lady with a short life, but her husbands were always

---

329) Yoshida, 1996, pp. 193–196.
330) Yoshida, 1996, pp. 196–197.
331) Kobayashi, 2011, p. 44.
332) Yoshida, 1996, pp. 196–197.
333) Fukuda, 2007, p. 31.

nice to her.

During her girlhood, Chacha, a well-off girl with a brilliant background was brought up with the love of her parents carefully and happily until Odani Castle was attacked and her father, Nagamasa, killed himself by *hara-kiri*. Before Nagamasa's death, Nobunaga told Nagamasa, "Because the Asakuras were bad, I had to fight with you but I have no grudge against you. I would not harm you if you abandoned your castle." However, Nagamasa never accepted it, saying, "I have no way out except killing myself since I was defeated." Nobunaga again approached Nagamasa, "I would give you a territory if you declared your loyally to me." But Nagamasa did not say "Yes." In those days, people thought that killing themselves by *hara-kiri* after losing in a war was a graceful loser's behavior. The warriors' world was not easy.[334]

What's more, before Nagamasa's death, Ichi and the three daughters were rescued from the castle. Nagamasa told Ichi, "I have decided to commit *hara-kiri*. Because you are Nobunaga's sister, Nobunaga would not hurt you. I'll send you back to him and be alive to dedicate the souls of the Azai family." Ichi responded, "I'd like to die with you. Continuing to be alive is shameful." However, Nagamasa kindly said to Ichi, "There are three daughters. Since they are women, Nobunaga wouldn't gain revenge against them. I don't want to kill them because they are innocent. Please go back to Nobunaga with our children to be alive." Ichi finally accepted what Nagamasa said, deciding to come back to Nobunaga with the three daughters. Before that, Nagamasa let two boys get away secretly because they were at risk of being murdered by Nobunaga. After Nagamasa made sure of the safety of his wife and children, he committed *hara-kiri* on August 28, 1573, when Chacha was still 4 years old.[335]

Regarding Chacha's brothers, Owada[336] said that she had three or four brothers although there are no exact documents mentioning about them.

---

334) Kuwata, 1958, pp. 19–20.
335) Kuwata 1958, pp. 20–22.
336) Owada 1997, pp. 39–40.

However, people usually confirm that she had two brothers. Although Nagamasa let the oldest Manpukumaru get away with his younger brother, after Nobunaga's intense chase finally, he was destroyed by Hideyoshi who was Nobunaga's subordinate warrior then. At that time, surviving boys were usually put to death because there were possibilities that the boys might get revenge against the person who killed their fathers. Nagamasa's second son, Manjumara (some call him Mankikumaru) was sent to a temple and later became a Buddhist priest.[337]

Chacha, her mother, and two sisters were sent to the residence of Oda Nobukane, a younger brother of Nobunaga, after Nagamasa's death. Nobunaga might wish to stay with them, but it was difficult for him to do so. Because he killed Nagamasa and the boy that the three daughters very much loved, they didn't want to live with Nobunaga in his castle. However, the four ladies, Ichi, Chacha, Hatsu, and Gō were still important relatives for Nobunaga. Although Ichi had the three daughters, she was young enough to get married again for Nobunaga's political reasons. In addition, the three daughters would also be used for political marriages and help Nobunaga in the future.[338] However, they seemed to live in Nobukane's residence without being attacked from anyone until Chacha was fourteen years old.

After Honnō-ji no Hen (the Honnō-ji Incident) in 1582, when Oda Nobunaga was killed by his subordinate warrior, Akechi Mitsuhide, on June 27th in 1582, a meeting in Kiyosu, the current Aichi Prefecture, was held in order to decide who was going to take over Nobunaga's position and how to distribute his territory. Although Nobunaga's first son was murdered with Nobunaga in the temple, the second and third son were still alive. Shibata Katsuie nominated the third son, Nobutaka, as the next leader since he was better than the second one in order to keep the Oda family going. However, Hideyoshi heavily defeated Akechi Mitsuhide before the meeting, recommending Sanhōshi (later,

---

337) Owada 1997, pp. 41–42.
338) Owada 1997, pp. 43–44.

Oda Hidenobu), who was three years old then and a son of Nobunaga's first son. Hideyoshi's recommendation was accepted and Hideyoshi's secret plot to wrestle the real power of politics from the Oda family seemed to go forward. The conflict between Katsuie and Hideyoshi was only getting larger and larger.[339]

After the Honnō-ji Incident, it was decided that Chacha with her two sisters move to the residence of Shibata Katsuie because of Ichi's remarriage with him. However, a happy life did not happen for a long time as the war between Katsuie and Hideyoshi started (the Battle of Shizugatake). Actually, the war was started by the third son of Nobunaga, Nobutaka, who did not like Hideyoshi obtaining power one by one, and Katsuie as a senior subordinate warrior of the Oda family. In April, 1583 finally, Katsuie's castle was besieged by Hideyoshi's squad, and Katsuie deciding to commit *hara-kiri* after recognizing his defeat. He held a large and gorgeous farewell party for an entire night and composed a death poem. Then, not only Katsuie and Ichi, but his entire family including his subordinate warriors, servants, and so forth, except for Chacha and her two sisters, more than eighty people killed themselves. In addition, the castle was wrapped up in flame and burned down. Chacha had lived with Katsuie for less than a year, losing her biological mother and the second father in her mid-teens. After losing her parents, Chacha and her two sisters were preserved by Hideyoshi who was an enemy of her second father and killed her brother Manpukumaru.[340]

Chacha's later news is not identified at all for a while until she became Hideyoshi's secondary wife, giving birth to a baby boy in 1589.[341] Owada[342] also relates that there is no literature talking about Chacha's sentiment on why she decided to become Hideyoshi's concubine, although her relatives were killed by Hideyoshi.

---

339) Owada 1997, pp. 49–50.
340) Kuwata 1958, pp. 29–32.
341) Kuwata 1958, pp. 33–34.
342) Owada 1997, p. 77.

However, Owada[343] guesses that Hideyoshi might use the approach that Chacha lost her hateful feelings against Hideyoshi. He seemed to love Chacha because she was similar to Ichi, whom he had romantic feelings of for a long time. After the youngest, Gō, married her cousin, and the marriage was already decided when Ichi had been alive,[344] Hideyoshi allowed Chacha and her sister Hatsu to have a gorgeous and luxurious life with first class food, clothing, and housing. This might have been very good for Chacha, having experienced on two occasions defeat and a miserable life. Next, Hatsu tied the knot with Kyōgoku Takatsugu, who became Hideoshi's subordinate warrior after the war in 1583[345] and Chacha's life in her residence was getting more and more beautiful. She might think her life was great in his housing and gradually was attracted to Hideyoshi who had authority.

Kobayashi describes that Chacha might have gradually fallen in love with Hideyoshi from the time of the cornerstone laying ceremony for the Colossal Hall of the Great Buddha in 1588. When Chacha recognized that Hideyoshi was trembling with fear from killing her relatives, her hate changed to pity and kindness.[346] Though, actually, we don't know the truth.

Then what kind of person was Toyotomi Hideyoshi, to have won Chacha's heart? It is said that he was born in 1537,[347] being from a poor famer's family or a son of a foot soldier. However, there is no exact information describing his birth. He gradually distinguished himself as a subordinate warrior of Oda Nobunaga around the age of twenty-eight when the Oda family grew by leaps and bounds. Hideyoshi was a brilliant warrior who achieved a very successful career in his life although he was from the bottom rung of the social ladder. After Azai Nagamasa died, at the age of thirty-six, Hideyoshi was given Odani Castle by Nobunaga, first time ever becoming a castellan. However, he moved

---

343) Owada 1997, pp. 78–79.
344) Kobayashi 2011, p. 61.
345) Kobayashi 2011, p. 61.
346) Kobayashi 2011, p. 62.
347) Some people say it was 1536.

76

from Odani to Nagahama where he built his castle and stayed there because locational conditions of Nagahama were better for the war than those of Odani. He always prepared perfectly for war by thorough observation and learning, and preparing the war purse with enough soldiers and money. Furthermore, we shouldn't forget his adept stratagems that his enemies sold out to him.

The most important event for Hideyoshi was the meeting in Kiyosu in 1582 after Oda Nobunaga killed himself in Honnō-ji due to the Akechi Mitsuhide uprising. At the meeting he helped Sanhōshi, only three years old then, take over Nobunaga's place and after that he defeated senior warriors of the Oda family one by one.

He then established a new position of the first-class subordinate warrior in the Oda family, in essence controlling the Oda administration in spite of ostensibly dedicating Sanhōshi. Although soon Hideyoshi came into conflict with politically strong Tokugawa Ieyasu, supporting Oda Nobukatsu, Nobunaga's second son, they eventually reconciled. In 1585, Hideyoshi began to attack Kishū, the existing Wakayama Prefecture, as well as the southern part of Mie Prefecture, Shikoku, now Kōchi, Tokushima, and Kagawa Prefectures and finally dominated those areas. Then Hideyoshi took up a post of kanpaku[348] that allowed him to make daimyōs follow his ideas as those from chōtei.[349] This implied that the relationship between Hideyoshi and the daimyōs was not just master and subordinates in warrior's world, but chōtei and people who served it. Hideyoshi's position was then at the top and he was no longer a subordinate warrior of the Oda family. In 1587, he controlled the Kyūshū district after prohibiting wars between warriors and defeating those who were against national law.[350] This is Hideyoshi's brief political background.

When it came to Hideyoshi's private life, he already had a legal wife whose name was Nene from Owari, now Aichi Prefecture. Regarding her name, some

---

348) A person conducting politics with the emperor whose position is the highest in Japan.
349) A political organ whose top was an emperor and held political power.
350) Ōishi 2020, pp. 124–157.

people call it One. Her birthday is not clear, but there are three possibilities: 1541, 1547, and 1548. Her father was Sugihara Sadaie and mother was Asahi, but she was adopted later by Asano Nagakatsu, her uncle, and Oda Nobunaga's subordinate warrior. Her mother Asahi opposed the marriage between Nene and Hideyoshi because he was from lower class society.[351] However, finally they were joined together. She was smart and a good wife, supporting and working for him since they were young. But they did not have children. Sooner or later Hideyoshi's women craze began.[352] It was so terrible that she took advice from Nobunaga in 1576, when Hideyoshi became a chatelain. Nobunaga praised Nene since she was always nice to him, saying "You are too good a wife for Hideyoshi. You should behave in a dignified and calm manner as a legal wife without caring about his mistresses." The relationship between Nene and Nobunaga seemed to be good and friendly.[353]

According to Kuwata,[354] Hideyoshi had sixteen mistresses next to Nene. Chacha was one of them. Because polygamy was allowed in those days, it might be natural for a powerful man like Hideyoshi to have them. They were Matsunomaru, Sanjō, Kaga, Sannomaru, Himeji, Kai, Otane, and so forth. Most of them were daughters from *daimyō* families. They became his subordinate warriors after being conquered by him. Defeated *daimyōs* pleaded for their daughters and sent them to him as an intention of surrender. For example, Kaga was a daughter of Maeda Toshiie who took the side of Shibata Katsuie at the Battle of Shizugatake, 1583, but became Hideyoshi's warrior after Katsuie was defeated. Some people say that he chose daughters from noble families because he was from lower class society. He might be a charming lady-killer. Although he had many mistresses, he had no children. Around that time, even if a lady made love with a man, she was not permitted to be his secondary wife, not

---

351) Fukuda 2007, p. 50.
352) At that time Hideyoshi was around forty years of age and was in the full vigor of manhood with economic power.
353) Kobayashi 2011, pp. 81–82.
354) Kuwata 1958, pp. 34–44.

receiving good treatment without giving birth to his baby.

Chacha with Oda Nagamasu, her uncle, and a tea master, moved from Osaka Castle to Yodo Castle[355] that was gorgeously renovated for her delivery in March, 1589. As around that time people of breeding didn't like the mess of birth, the delivery was usually held in a different place from the main house.[356] Regarding the wife of a husband with a lot of authority, a great place was prepared for having a baby and the place was called delivery housing. After that, she came to be presented with Yodo no Kata, a person in Yodo or Yodo-dono, Mrs. Yodo.[357]

On the 27th of May, 1589, Yodo-dono gave birth to a brilliant baby boy at the age of 20. On the other hand, Hideyoshi was around fifty. Both of them were so happy, naming him Sute (abandon) because at that time people said abandoned children grew well. By and by his name was changed to Tsurumatsu, a happy name meaning long life. Since Hideyoshi was a *kanpaku*, many court nobles in Kyoto and *daimyōs* sent him deluxe gifts with celebratory statements. About four months later after Sute (Tsurumatsu) was born, Yodo-dono and he were moved to Osaka Castle by Hideyoshi. It was a ceremony telling people that the Toyotomi Family had an heir, Tsurumatsu, taking over the Toyotomi administration. On New Year's Day in 1590 many court nobles in Kyoto visited Tsurumatsu with rich presents in order to give him greeting of the New Year, which implied to kiss up to Hideyoshi. In February, Hideyoshi had Tsurumatsu meet his legal wife, Kita no Mandokoro (Nene), and Ōmandokoro, Hideyoshi's biological mother.[358]

According to Fukuda,[359] Hideyoshi distributed 6,000 gold and 25,000 silver pieces to temples and *daimyōs* before Tsurumatsu's birth because he

---

355) Yodo Castle was located at the place where the River Uji, the River Katsura, and the River Kizu were connected together in current Kyoto city but it is gone now.
356) It was also that people were careful about Nene without her biological children living in Osaka Castle.
357) Owada 1997, pp. 80–82.
358) Kuwata 1958, pp. 50–51.
359) Fukuda 2007, p. 90.

wanted them to understand that he was the biological father of the coming baby, using financial power. Since Hideyoshi did not have any biological children at all, in spite of having a lot of mistresses, people thought he didn't produce his own sperm. Yodo-dono's pregnancy surprised them, some suspecting that the baby's father was not Hideyoshi. It was also an advance celebration.

In April, 1590, Hideyoshi began an attack on Odawara Castle located in the current Kanagawa Prefecture, but he always had Tsurumatsu on his mind, sending a letter to Kita no Mandokoro which said, "I'd like to see Tsurumatsu very much but I have to fight now to unify the nation and make it peaceful. Because the war is going to take time, I'd like to call the wives of my warriors and Chacha over to Odawara. Ask Yodo-dono to visit Odawara, etc." From this letter we recognize that Hideyoshi did not have Kita no Mandokoro take a back seat to Yodo-dono because he asked Kita no Mandokoro to help Yodo-dono make a call there without secretly inviting her. She then went to him in Odawara with some warriors to assist her, leaving Tsurumatsu in Osaka since children of people in high positions had many servants who took care of them.[360] Because the war took so much time, Hideyoshi built a castle over a very short time in order to show himself capable of defeating his enemy and to relax his warriors. In the castle he held tea ceremonies and drinking parties with his warriors, including Yodo-dono, and their wives.[361]

On July 5th finally Hideyoshi felled Odawara Castle and soon headed into Ōu district, containing the existing Aomori, Iwate, Akita, Miyagi, Fukushima, and Iwate Prefectures, to dominate and unify them, having Yodo-dono return to her residence before leaving for the Ōu district. After finishing this work in Ōu, he carried out the national unification, returning with glory to Jurakutei[362] in Kyoto. Because Yodo-dono was in Yodo Castle, he sent a letter to her. It

360) Kuwata 1958, pp. 51–54.
361) Ōishi 2020, pp. 158–159.
362) In 1586, Hideyoshi began to build Jurakutei where he lived and conducted politics, but it was finished in 1587.

said, "I guess you worry about me because I didn't write to you after leaving you at Odawara. Did Tsurumatsu grow and are you fine? Be careful about fires and keep the place organized. I'm going back to you around the 20th, looking forward to holding Turumatsu in my arms."[363]

Yodo-dono and Hideyoshi very much cherished their son. When Tsurumatsu was around three years old, he began to learn a dance, enjoying it. Hideyoshi, doting on his child, soon returned mail to Tsurumatsu after Hideyoshi received a letter from him. The letter went, "I heard you learned a dance. It is good. Practice it hard. I will come and see you soon." Not only Yodo-dono but Kita no Mandokoro having no biological children also devoted a lot of attention to him because he was an important heir of the Toyotomi administration.[364]

After Yodo-dono delivered Tsurumatsu, an heir of Toyotomi Hideyoshi, a *kanpaku*, her position was stronger, and she desired to make a personal statement with confidence and latitude, although she had been quiet before. Her first personal statement was that she wanted to hold a memorial service for her biological parents, Azai Nagamasa and Ichi, although Nagamasa was Hideyoshi's enemy before.[365] The reasons why Nagamasa asked Ichi to stay alive with her three children when he was dying were not only that he very much loved them but that he wanted them to hold memorial services for the Azai family. Ichi prayed for the repose of Nagamasa's soul until she died. The reason Ichi left the three daughters when killing herself with her second husband was also that she wanted them to dedicate the souls of the Azai family. Yodo-dono well understood them.[366] Ichi's seventh and Nagamasa's seventeenth anniversaries of death were in 1589 when Yodo-dono delivered Tsurumatsu. Because having a baby boy was a real achievement in those days, Hideyoshi, who did not have any children until then was so happy and might

363) Kuwata 1958, pp. 56–59.
364) Kuwata 1958, pp. 60–61.
365) Owada 1997, p. 85.
366) Kuwata 1958, pp. 82–83.

accept Yodo-dono's request. At that time Yodo-dono ordered an artist to draw their pictorial images for the memorial service and they are still now in Jimyōin, a temple on Mt. Kōya.[367] In 1594, on Nagamasa's twenty-first anniversary of death, she built a family temple[368] in Kyoto named Yōgenin that was the same as his posthumous Buddhist name, Hideyoshi donating a large tract of land for the temple. Although establishing the temple must have been her earnest wish for a long time, the temple was later lost in a fire. After Yodo-dono's death in 1621, the temple was rebuilt by her youngest sister, Gō, a legal wife of Tokugawa Hidetada, and whenever it was repaired, Tokugawa Shogunate covered its expenditure.[369] The sisters from the Azai family then kept this promise with their parents.

Unfortunately, Tsurumatsu was frail. In November, 1589, because Tsurumatsu was sick, a doctor visited and stayed with him for a month. In January, 1590, since Tsurumatsu was not yet recovered, Hideyoshi inquired after his health. Whenever Tsurumatsu was in poor condition, people asked priests in temples and shrines to pray for his recovery.[370] In January, 1591 he felt ill but recovered after being giving an invocation as usual. However, in August he was very sick and getting worse and worse, finally passing away although famous doctors were invited to give him medicine in addition to prayer.[371] His funeral was held in Myōshin-ji in Kyoto and his ashes were placed in Tōfuku-ji, Kyoto where Hideyoshi and many people, including his servants mourned.[372] Hideyoshi built Shōun-ji in Kyoto and donated Tsurumatsu's mementos, such as his sword, suit of feudal armour, toys, etc.[373]

In 1591, after Tsurumatsu's death, Hideyoshi decided to transfer his

---

367) Owada 1997, pp. 85–86.
368) In Japan, one family has one grave, and they are in the same grave after their death.
369) Kuwata 1958, pp. 84–86.
370) Fukuda 2007, p. 117.
371) Owada 1997, p. 90.
372) Fukuda 2007, p. 119.
373) Kuwata 1958, p. 63.

position, *kanpaku* to Hidetsugu, his nephew, becoming a *taikō*[374] and preparing to send troops to Korea. Because Hideyoshi also gave over Jurakutei, where politics were conducted, to Hidetsugu, Nene moved to Osaka Castle.[375]

Hideyoshi began to build Hizennagoya Castle in the current Saga Prefecture as a hub for sending troops to Korea, coming to the castle from Jurakutei in Kyoto with Yodo-dono on the 26th of March, 1592 after receiving the information that the castle was almost completed. Although going to the castle where warriors prepared to head into the battlefield was not permitted with women present a little while back, the rule was changed in the epoch of Hideyoshi. Because he had won the Battle of Odawara with Yodo-dono, he decided to take her with him. Hideyoshi not only took Yodo-dono but his other concubines as well to have a sightseeing tour, and it took them a long time to get there. They probably stayed at the castle until about the end of the year.[376]

Around that time, Hideyoshi's mother was sick, very much worrying about Hideyoshi attacking Korea. In May, 1592 he sent her a letter from Hizennagoya Castle in order to offer her comfort after recognizing that she wasn't able to eat enough because of her old age and being concerned for him. The letter said, "I'm fine with eating enough food. You also enjoy eating. Don't worry about me…" In July he received news that his mother was very seriously ill. He decided to go back to Jurakutei in Kyoto so as to speak with her one last time after arranging the strategy of the war. However, on his way to Jurakutei he knew that his mother passed away on the 22nd of July. Hideyoshi was so depressed by the death of his mother, but continued to Kyoto anyway and came back to Hizennagoya after finishing her funeral and praying sincerely for the repose of her soul.[377]

Yodo-dono had painfully experienced the death of her parents and felt

---

374) *Taikō* was the position of a person who transferred over his place, *kanpaku* to someone (usually his son).
375) Fukuda 2007, pp. 120–121.
376) Owada 1997, pp. 91–92.
377) Kobayashi 2011, pp. 96–98 and p. 101.

sympathetic toward Hideyoshi making efforts to advance in the world so as to please his mother. Hideyoshi cried and cried because it was his first time to lose his parent.[378] Her sympathy changed into love and as a result, she was expecting again after Tsurumatsu's death. Soon she went back to Osaka Castle.[379]

Hideyoshi, knowing about Yodo-dono's pregnancy from Nene's letter, wrote back to Nene. In the letter he described first the amicable settlement between the emperor of China and Hideyoshi after occupying the capitol in Korea, and then that he was going back to Osaka in July or August. Then he talked about Yodo-dono's expecting. Although he mentioned it was happy, it hadn't hit him yet and he still seemed not to be able to recover from the shock of Tsurumatsu's death.[380]

When Yodo-dono had Tsurumatsu, Yodo Castle was renovated as delivery housing. But in the case of her next child, neither Hideyoshi nor Yodo-dono prepared housing, probably because they thought they were unlucky owing to Tsurumatsu's death. Yodo-dono was then at Osaka Castle.[381]

On the 3rd of August, 1593, Yodo-dono gave birth to a baby boy in Osaka Castle. After receiving the news of the baby from his subordinate warrior, Hideyoshi still being in Hizennagoya wrote a letter to Nene. The letter said, "I'm happy with the news told by my warrior. I named the baby Hiroi[382] (picking up). Soon I'm coming back." The origin of the name, Hiroi, was from picking up the baby after he was once abandoned because in those days people said that abandoned children grew well. Actually, Hideyoshi left Hizennagoya on August 15th and arrived at Osaka on the 25th meeting his baby. He must have been so happy.[383]

378) There are almost no resources talking about his father.
379) Kobayashi 2011, pp. 101–103.
380) Kuwata 1958, pp. 69–70.
381) Owada 1997, pp. 92–93.
382) Later his name changed to Hideyori.
383) Kuwata 1958, pp. 70–72.

After Hiroi's birth we can see Hideyoshi doting on his son. He sometimes sent a letter to Yodo-dono to ask about how Hiroi was doing when he was not able to see him. On October, 1593 a letter said, "Give Hiroi enough mother's milk and help him to sleep alone. You should also eat enough nutritious food so that you can give him good milk. I'll see you soon." Hideyoshi also got a toy that Hiroi liked from a foreign country. What Hideyoshi called Hiroi in the letters eventually changed from Hiroi to Ohiro and Mr. Ohiroi, which lends us to understand that Hideyoshi very much loved his son because what Hideyoshi called him was getting more courteous.[384]

Regarding Yodo-dono, the biological mother of Hiroi whose father was *taikō*, she was treated hospitably and graciously. Around 1593, smallpox became prevalent and unfortunately, she was affected by the disease. Because Hideyoshi was concerned about her very much, he ordered all temples and shrines in Japan to pray for her recovery while donating a lot of rice.[385] Since in the case of a severe condition people lost their life and they would have pockmarks on their skin if they didn't die, they were afraid of the disease at that time. Fortunately, she recovered without any pockmarks. Although she was sick for a while, she was happy with giving birth to, cherishing and bringing up her son with Hideyoshi. She came to have more power than any other concubines after delivering, and was allowed to do anything she wanted to with a luxurious life.[386]

The relationship between Kita no Mandokoro (Nene), Hideyoshi's legal wife, and Yodo-dono seems to have been ok although there is some information talking about their strained relationship. Regarding the position between Kita no Mandokoro and Yodo-dono, the position of Kita no Mandokoro was higher than that of Yodo-dono's even though Yodo-dono gave birth to an heir of the Toyotomi government and was from the family whose place was much higher

384) Kuwata 1958, pp. 74–80.
385) In those days rice was more valuable than money.
386) Kuwata 1958, pp. 76–81.

than that of Kita no Mandokoro.[387] Around that time, concubines understood that there were big differences between the legal wife and a concubine, taking off their hats to her. It was an unspoken rule. Actually, Kita no Mandokoro was a mature and well-balanced lady. In addition, Hideyoshi usually saved Kita no Mandokoro's face and did not call Yodo-dono over to his place during the battle without first telling Kita no Mandokoro. In 1594, when they watched cherry blossoms at Osaka Castle, Kita no Mandokoro was in the first place, Yodo-dono was the second. Although the treatment towards both of them was especially good compared with other secondary wives, Hideyoshi always put Kita no Mandokoro first and Yodo-dono second.[388] Kita no Mandokoro took Hiroi under her wing and he sent a letter paying his respects to her even after Hideyoshi's death without being bothered by his mother. From this condition the relationship between Kita no Mandokoro and Yodo-dono was fine.[389]

Let's go back to the birth of Hiroi (later, Hideyori). Although it was a celebratory occasion for Yodo-dono and Hideyoshi, a problem occurred for them. The problem was that Hideyoshi gave his sister's son, Hidetsugu, adopted by Hideyoshi himself, the position of *kanpaku* and Jurakutei where politics was carried out. After Tsurumatsu's death, disappointed Hideyoshi decided to retire, moving over the position of *kanpaku* to Hidetsugu because Hideyoshi thought that he would never have another biological son. In August, 1592 he began to build Fushimi Castle where he was supposed to enjoy the rest of his life. However, in August the following year Hideyori was born and then Hideyoshi changed his mind, wanting Hideyori to take over his position. Hideyoshi established an extremely gorgeous castle that overpowered Hidetsugu because in fact, Hideyoshi wanted to pass the castle on to his son. The chasm between Hideyoshi and Hidetsugu started when Hidetsugu began to

---

387) At that time a baby from a mother whose family position was low, would have a difficult time achieving a successful career.

388) Fukuda 2007, pp. 50–52.

389) Kuwata 1958, p. 109.

recognize that he was being treated like a burden.[390]

Here the paper introduces Hidetsugu a little bit to the readers. Although there is some information talking about Toyotomi Hidetsugu in *Taikōsama Gunki*, it doesn't have a favorable view of him. For example, it said, "When the present *kanpaku* (Hidetsugu) was a child, his name was Hashiba Hidetsugu. Since he is a nephew of Hideyoshi, the former *kanpaku*, and without great accomplishments, Hidetsugu took over the management of Hachimanyama Castle before at the age of twenty, with no interruption ruling the Owari district at the age of twenty-three. He was promoted smoothly. When he was twenty-six, he was moved over to the position of *kanpaku* and Jurakutei where he had a lot of beautiful concubines live and enjoyed a luxurious life.[391] This implies that although Hidetsugu was incompetent, he was successful in life owing to Hideyoshi. Another piece of information from *Taikōsama Gunki* described, "Hidetsugu was hunting Japanese deer on Mt. Hiei in the current Kyoto Prefecture where hunting was prohibited. Although Buddhist priests there told him not to hunt, he did not accept what they said and ate the meat of animals, harassing the priests.[392] Here also, Hidetsugu was described as a tyrannical leader killing animals.[393] There are some people that assert that the contents of the book were written by an author taking the side of Hideyoshi and are lacking in reliability because the author tried to create a story that was convenient for Hideyoshi.

Before long, the birth of Hideyori (Hiroi) also brought Hidetsugu tragedy. After Yodo-dono and Hideyoshi moved to Fushimi Castle, he began to work out stratagem to dislodge Hidetsugu from the position of power. On July 3, 1595, Hidetsugu was interviewed in connection with a plot against the regime, though in fact there is no information left about the content of interview and plot.

---

390) Owada 1997, pp. 98–100.
391) Kobayashi 2011, p. 107.
392) Owada 1997, p. 101.
393) Killing creatures, not only human beings but animals, was the worst deed in the Buddhist world.

Investigators who knew Hideyoshi's intention, standing by his side, decided that Hidetsugu plotted treachery. On July 8, Hidetsugu was called to Fushimi Castle and deprived of his position of *kanpaku* by Hideyoshi. Furthermore, Hideyoshi ordered Hidetsugu to become a Buddhist priest at Mt. Kōya in the existing Wakayama Prefecture, and later to commit *hara-kiri*. What's more, Hideyoshi might have gone insane, because Hidetsugu's legal wife, concubines, children, a total of thirty-nine people were killed in Kyoto and Jyurakutei where Hidetsugu lived. Hideyoshi might only have wanted Hideyori to take over his position.[394]

At the same time when Hidetsugu's affair occurred, Hideyoshi had all *daimyōs* promise that: 1. They had to protect Hideyori without hiding anything. 2. They had to follow what Hideyoshi decided. 3. If you didn't treat Hideyori nicely or didn't follow Hideyoshi, you, including your relatives, would have to receive punishment. Hideyoshi was getting older and sick. He might have had a premonition that he would be close to the end of his life. He was very much concerned about Hideyori.[395]

Hideyoshi began to be sick and was laid up in spring, 1598 after he watched cherry blossoms near Daigo-ji in Kyoto with many people. On June 16th he visited Kongōbu-ji on Mt. Kōya, the current Wakayama Prefecture, which brought him a serious condition.[396] On August 5, 1598 Hideyoshi, finally knowing that his death was close at hand, left his will. He picked out five *daimyōs* managing politics and five of his senior warriors performing practical tasks to set up the consultation system.[397] The five *daimyōs*[398] were: Tokugawa Ieyasu, Maeda Toshiie, Ukita Hideie, Uesugi Kagekatsu, and Mōri Terumoto, and the five warriors[399] from the Toyotomi Family were: Natsuka[400] Masaie,

---

394) Owada 1997, p. 102–103.
395) Kuwata 1958, pp. 97–98.
396) Owada 1997, p. 134.
397) It was the best authorities of the central government, the Tokugawa administration.
398) 徳川家康、前田利家、宇喜多秀家、上杉景勝、毛利輝元
399) 長束正家、石田三成、増田長盛、浅野長政、前田玄似
400) Some people say, "Nagatsuka"

Ishida Mitsunari, Mashita Nagamori, Asano Nagamasa, and Maeda Geni. Hideyoshi asked Tokugawa Ieyasu and his son, Hidetada, Hideyori's father-in-law[401] to cover the political administration at Fushimi Castle, looking after Hideyori until he became an adult. Hideyoshi also requested Maeda Toshiie to take care of various things related to Hideyori at Osaka Castle. Hideyoshi had Ukita Hideie work as a bridge between the five *daimyōs* and the five warriors from the Toyotomi Family. Hideyoshi wanted the ten people to help Hideyori until he grew up, taking over the Toyotomi administration after his death. On the 18th of August, Hideyoshi breathed his last breath in Fushimi Castle. Many people were by his bedside when he passed away. He was in his sixty-second year.[402]

In April of the following year, Yodo-dono and Hideyori, who had been in Fushimi Castle moved to Osaka Castle in deference to Hideyoshi's will. Fushimi Castle was a place for Hideyoshi's retirement and Osaka Castle was that for politics. When Yodo-dono and her son began to live in Osaka Castle, Kita no Mandokoro, Nene, Hideyoshi's legal wife, moved to a residence in Kyoto and in 1603 she entered a nunnery praying for Hideyoshi. Yodo-dono had to foster Hideyori who was still small, helping his administration as his assistant, though Tokugawa Ieyasu was asked to manage politics.[403]

Although Hideyoshi chose the five *daimyōs* and the five senior warriors from the Toyotomi Family to help Hideyori until he grew up, taking over Hideyoshi's position, soon a problem occurred after the death of Maeda Toshiie, one of the five *daimyōs*. He supported Hideyori in Osaka Castle, contributing to keep harmony among the ten people. After his death his son, Maeda Toshinaga, took over his place. At the same time when Maeda Toshiie passed away, Ishida Mitsunari was attacked by Toyotomi's warriors who were against him. As a result, he fell from the position. Because of Toshiie's death and Mitsunari's

---

401) Hideyori's legal wife was Tokugawa Hidetada's daughter, Sen.
402) Fukuda 2007, pp. 162–164.
403) Owada 1997, pp. 137–138.

downfall, the system of the five *daimyōs* and five Toyotomi warriors began to collapse.[404]

After the death of Maeda Toshiie, Tokugawa Ieyasu began to develop his strategies, trying to hold onto the real power. This was the beginning of the Battle of Sekigahara in 1600. The five new *daimyōs* put out the message saying that the *daimyōs* in Osaka and Kyoto could go back to their territories (hometowns) so as to do their jobs there.[405] Because of this message, Maeda Toshinaga and Uesugi Kagekatsu went back to their lands to work there. However, Toshinaga's behavior was called rebellion because the Maeda family had to take a responsibility for affairs in Osaka Castle. Although Toshiie told his son to work in Osaka for three years without coming back to his country, Toshinaga didn't follow it owing to Ieyasu's recommendation that he could go home. This was Ieyasu's strategy to frame Toshinaga. This case was settled after Toshinaga's mother was sent to the Tokugawa Family as a hostage. However, the equal relationship between the Maeda family and the Tokugawa Family was broken. Soon Ieyasu moved to Osaka Castle in spite of Hideyoshi's will that Ieyasu needed to work in Fushimi Castle. In fact, at that time Osaka Castle was the center for managing the Tokugawa administration. Ieyasu was getting more power.[406]

Furthermore, next, Tokugawa Ieyasu focused on the Uesugi family whose top was Kagekatsu going back to his home. As soon as Kagekatsu arrived at his home, Ieyasu requested Kagekatsu to return to Kyoto. Now after Hideyoshi's death he had visited Osaka and Kyoto, staying there for about one year and he almost didn't cover the jobs for his country, so he did not accept Ieyasu's request. Then Ieyasu decided to put down the Uesugi family because he was a fill-in of Hideyoshi. Kagekatsu didn't accept Ieyasu's request, which implied

---

404) Yabe 2014, pp. 84–85.
405) Although *Daimyōs* (feudal lords) were gathered, living in Osaka and Kyoto in order to work for the emperor, court nobles, and in this case Hideyoshi, they sometimes needed to go back to their own territories to cover the jobs there.
406) Yabe 2014, p. 85.

that Kagekatsu acted counter to Hideyoshi.[407] Before attacking the Uesugi family, Ieyasu visited Hideyori to tell him that the attack would be justice in order to protect the Toyotomi administration. Ieyasu was given a lot of gold and rice as a going away gift by Hideyori.[408] However, the important thing for Ieyasu was not Kagekatsu's returning to Kyoto but leaving Osaka so that an anti-Ieyasu power in Osaka and Kyoto was able to prepare for fighting with Ieyasu during his leaving. Ieyasu wanted to defeat anti-Ieyasu power and hold all the power to manage the Toyotomi government. As Ieyasu expected, anti-Ieyasu power, including Maeda Geni, Mashita Nagamori, and Natsuka Masaie from the five Toyotomi warriors, and Ukita Hideie and Mōri Terumoto from the five *daimyōs* impeached Ieyasu because he tracked down Ishida Mitsunari and Asano Nagamasa, and also attacked Maeda Toshinaga and Uesugi Kagekatsu. They also asserted that Ieyasu tried to cripple the system of the five *daimyōs* and five Toyotomi warriors, which was against Hideyoshi. Ieyasu was then isolated himself. Owing to this, their relationship grew worse.[409] A battle related to a split among friends under the Toyotomi administration was going to happen.

On September 15th in 1600 the Battle of Sekigahara occurred between the East squad whose top was Tokugawa Ieyasu and the West squad whose leader was Ishida Mitsunari[410]. Until the early afternoon of the day, the whereabouts of the battle were not identified. However, because Kobayakawa Hideaki[411] from the West squad switched sides, attacking the West, it woke up a debacle. In the afternoon some warriors in the West squad ran away to different places and in the evening the East squad got a big win. It was a big war involving all east-west *daimyōs*. After the war, Tokugawa Ieyasu became an actual ruler

---

407) Yabe 2014, p. 86.
408) Miyamoto 1999, p. 166.
409) Yabe 2014, pp. 86–87.
410) A recent view is that the West squad's leader is not Ishida Mitsunari but MōriTerumoto.
411) Kobayakawa Hideaki was a nephew of Nene. Once he was adopted by the Toyotomi Family as Hideyoshi's successor but he was sent to the Kobayakawa family as an adopted son after Hideyori's birth.

reigning over the whole nation.[412]

Although after the Battle of Sekigahara Tokugawa, Ieyasu actually held the real power, the power relationship between the Toyotomi Family and the Tokugawa Family did not change soon. Ieyasu was still a daimyō under the Toyotomi administration. Yodo-dono thought the war occurred not because of the split between the Toyotomi and the Tokugawa but owing to Ishida Mitsunari's rebellion.[413] She seemed to believe that Hideyori was going to take over Hideyoshi's position after he grew up, with Ieyasu being a surrogate for a while.[414] She should have understood the custom of the civil war period that a kingmaker depredated the administration after Hideyoshi's death as Hideyoshi took the Oda administration.[415]

On New Year's Day in 1603, various *daimyōs* visited Hideyori in Osaka Castle to say New Year's greetings and the next day they called on Ieyasu in Fushimi Castle to do the same thing. This implied that Hideyori's position was higher than that of Ieyasu, Yodo-dono wanting to continue the situation until Hideyori reached the age of fifteen, when he grew up and succeeded the Hideyoshi's place.[416]

However, in February, 1603 Tokugawa Ieyasu was conferred the position of a *seiitaishogun* by *chōtei*[417] and opened the Tokugawa Shogunate in Edo, the current Tokyo, which meant that the relation of a master (Toyotomi) and a servant (Tokugawa) was revered. Before becoming the *seiitaishogun,* Ieyasu visited Osaka to give Hideyori greetings of the New Year. However, at this point, even if Hideyori sent an envoy to Ieyasu in Fushimi to give him greetings

412) Kobayashi 2011, p. 188.
413) Ōishi 2020, p. 195.
414) Kuwata 1958, p. 119.
415) Owada 1997, p. 158.
416) Owada 1997, p. 162–163.
417) *seiitaishogun* (Barbarian Subduing Generalissimo). It was the highest official position of warriors given by *chōtei* (a political organ whose top level was an emperor which seized political power at that time).

of it, Ieyasu did not even reply.[418]

After the Battle of Sekigahara, Yodo-dono as Hideyori's mother had to foster him by herself as he was still so small.[419] According to Fukuda,[420] owing to her over protection and favoritism, he was spoiled although there was another opinion that he was not. She was always with him, not leaving him even for a moment, having him enjoy the *kabuki* (traditional drama performed by male actors), dance, music, and so forth. As a result, he became a person who did not know much of the world. Actually, he was learned in office organizations, laws, wars, *wakas* (traditional Japanese poems), and Confucian, but seemed to lack martial arts as a warrior.

Furthermore, Yodo-dono had to take up the household management, including Hideyoshi's huge inheritance property, spending a lot of money on repairing and building shrines and temples under the name of Toyotomi Hideyori. Yodo-dono was a devout believer in Buddhist and Shinto deities. Hideyoshi started to establish temples such as Enryaku-ji, now in Shiga Prefecture, Kongōbu-ji in Wakayama Prefecture, Hongan-ji in Kyoto Prefecture, Daigo-ji in Kyoto and so forth, Hideyori taking them over after Hideyoshi's death. In addition, temples and shrines related to Hideyoshi covered Osaka, Nara, Mie, Shimane Prefectures, etc. Hōkokubyō, in the current Kyoto Prefecture, Hōkoku-ji, Kyoto, and the Osaka Toyokuni Shrine was newly built but almost a hundred other temples and shrines were rebuilt and repaired, which began in 1598.[421] Some examples are following.

In 1601, the main hall of Yamato Hōkadō (a temple), in the current Nara Prefecture was actually rebuilt by Yodo-dono's wish although it was rebuilt under the name of Hideyori.[422]

418) Kuwata 1958, pp. 118–119.
419) Madeda Toshie passed away and Tokugawa Ieyasu gave up the place as one of the five *daimyōs*.
420) Fukuda 2007, pp. 181–182.
421) Fukuda 2014, p. 117.
422) Fukuda 2007, pp. 183–184.

In 1602, the chapel of Ōmi Ishiyamadera now in Shiga Prefecture, was renovated by Yodo-dono who wanted to prevent her and her family from bad tidings.[423]

In 1607, because Kōdaiin[424] asked Hideyori (Yodo-dono) to set up Kitano Shrine in Osaka, it was built.[425]

She also constructed a new bridge in Keikōin[426] (a temple) in Ise, the existing Mie Prefecture, because the ex-bridge was destroyed by a fire in 1601. She took tremendous care of the temple because in days of old the Azai family financially supported it, too.[427] What's more, when Hideyoshi was still alive, he asked the temple congregation to pray for Hideyori's health, success, and so on spending much money.[428] She also donated a lot of money and things to the temple.[429]

On the 28th of July in 1603, Sen, who was a fiancé of Hideyori, moved to Osaka castle with her servants. She was a granddaughter of Ieyasu and her biological mother was Gō, Yodo-dono's youngest sister. Sen was born in 1597, at that time being in her seventh year and Hideyori was in his eleventh year. Gō worried about little Sen visiting Osaka Castle from Edo, staying at Osaka for a while. Although the Tokugawa Family was not happy with their marriage, it was a promise between Hideyoshi and Ieyasu before Hideyoshi's death. The two mothers, Yodo-dono and Gō, made an effort to complete it so that the Toyomomi Family and the Tokugawa Family kept a good relationship. In 1606, Sen in her sixteenth year underwent a rite of womanhood and became Hideyori's wife.[430]

---

423) Fukuda 2007, pp. 182–183.
424) Kōdaiin is Nene's name after she became a nun.
425) Fukuda 2007, p. 185.
426) In 1869, Keikōin was abolished with almost one hundred temples in Ise, and in 1872, Ise Shrine bought it, now becoming a religious institution.
427) Fukuda 2007, pp. 185.
428) Fukuda 2014, p. 118.
429) Fukuda 2007, p. 183.
430) Fukuda 2007, pp. 173–175, p. 177. Fukuda 2014, p. 113.

In 1605, Tokugawa Ieyasu moved over the position of the shogun to his son, Hidetada, and he was conferred the position of a *seiitaishogun* by *chōtei*.[431] This demonstrated the durability of the Tokugawa administration in the world, trying to give up the recovery of the Toyotomi administration. Soon Ieyasu encouraged Hideyori to visit Hidetada to give him words for celebration.[432] However, because it meant that the Toyotomi Family would become a *daimyō* under the Tokugawa administration, Yodo-dono rejected Ieyasu's request, saying, "If you make Hideyori visit Hidetada, I would kill Hideyori and myself."[433] She never accepted Ieyasu's request.

When the power of the Tokugawa Shogunate was getting stronger, the matter related to the inscription on a bell at Hōkō-ji occurred in 1614. Hōkō-ji was built by Hideyoshi saying, "There should be the Great Buddha in Kyoto Prefecture too, in addition to Nara." Although it took almost nine years to finish it up, the Great Buddha was destroyed by an earthquake the following year. Then it was rebuilt, burning down again, and rebuilding again. Then the Tokugawa Shogunate focused on the temple bell that was completed with the Great Buddha, complaining, "The inscription on the bell implies the Toyotomi Family's prosperity but the Tokugawa's misfortune." The start of the matter was when a monk, associated with the Tokugawa Shogunate, presented the inscription on the temple bell meant to bring unhappiness and disasters to the Tokugawa government.[434]

This was definitely an unjustified complaint of Tokugawa Ietasu, who wanted to keep the Toyotomi Family under the rule of the Tokugawa administration. Because the side of the Toyotomi did not have evil intentions

---

431) Although Ieyasu nominally retired, living in Sunpu Castle, in the current Shizuoka Prefecture, in fact he controlled the government and Hidetada just enforced what Ieyasu decided.

432) Actually Kōdaiin, Nene was a messenger to tell Hideyori and Yodo-dono to visit Hidetada for the celebration. In 1590, when Hidetada was eleven years old, he was sent to Jurakutei as a hostage, seeing Hideyoshi. At that time his name changed from Nagamatsu to Hidetada taking a part of the name of Hideyoshi. Nene took him under her wing and he grew up in Jurakutei.

433) Kuwata 1958, pp. 121–122.

434) Ōishi 2020, pp. 197–198.

against Ieyasu, soon Katagiri Katsumoto was sent to Ieyasu to excuse the matter. However, he took the time to see Ieyasu and Yodo-dono, running out of patience, send two women with high position to Ieyasu. Ieyasu was nice to the women saying, "You don't have to worry about that." However, from senior warriors in the Tokugawa government, Katagiri Katsumoto took back a message stating: "1. Hideyori should leave Osaka Castle and move to another place. 2. Hideyori like other *daimyōs* should live in Edo, now Tokyo, and his territory should shift. 3. Yodo-dono should be sent to the Tokugawa Family as a hostage. Yodo-dono must choose one of them." Because the content of the message was very different from what the two women said, Katagiri Katsumoto was referred to as a betrayer, before long leaving the Toyotomi Family.[435] Ieyasu might use the two different messages in order to make the Toyotomis confused or he hadn't decided what to do. If Yodo-dono accepted one of the conditions, he might be satisfied because it implied the Toyotomi Family became a *daimyō* under the Tokugawa government. However, she never did. Because she was born as a niece of a ruler, Oda Nobunaga, who almost reigned over the entire country, a wife of Toyotomi Hideyoshi, a *kanpaku,* and a mother of Hideyori who might become a ruler of the whole nation, she was not able to allow herself to follow Ieyasu's request.[436]

On October 2, 1614, Tokugawa Ieyasu deciding to attack the Toyotomi Family left Sunpu Castle, in the present Shizuoka Prefecture, and moved to Kyoto, while the side of the Toyotomis also began to prepare for war, buying a lot of rice and gunpowder. Yodo-dono and Toyotomi Hideyori gathered almost 100,000 masterless warriors, although *daimyōs* related to the Toyotomi administration did not help them, except for Sanada Yukimura, Chōsokabe Morichika, etc. On November 26, Osaka Fuyu no Jin (the Winter Siege of Osaka) started. Ieyasu's troops were 200,000. However, it was difficult for Ieyasu to assault Osaka Castle because it was enclosed by moats. Moreover,

---

435) Fukuda 2007, pp. 209–214.
436) Ōishi 2020, p. 201.

Sanada Yukimura very much contributed to disturbing the incursion of the Tokugawa troops by building his castle to protect Osaka Castle. Because of the hard battle that ensued, Ieyasu considered burying the hatchet with the Toyotomi Family.[437]

Before a negotiation for peace would commence, Ieyasu took a strategy that would ensure its success. A cannon salvo occurred on December 16th, which was a warning shot. Because he aimed at the place where Yodo-dono stayed with many female servants, it was very effective. As the warning shot was struck by lightning, seven or eight female servants were killed and girls were crying. There were about 10,000 women there. Furthermore, Ieyasu's squad started to dig a tunnel toward Osaka Castle, which also made people scared. In addition, since shots and gunpowder began to be exhausted, the side of Yodo-dono accepted the negotiation.[438]

Tokugawa Ieyasu asked Jōkōin Hatsu who was a younger sister of Yodo-dono and older sister of Gō, the youngest sister of Yodo-dono and a legal wife of Hidetada, Ieyasu's son, to arrange the peace negotiation because Jōkōin related to both sides. Moreover, she was a nun. In this era, Buddhist priests were often selected to assist in this type of negotiation because they broke with the world where various interests and earthly desires existed. Although the first meeting was held between Jōkōin, a representative of Yodo-dono's side, which was the West squad, and Acha no Tsubone, that of Ieyasu's, the East squad, it didn't reach a settlement owing to the big gap between their requests. On December 19th, the second meeting was held and they reached a settlement, deciding: 1. While the main room in Osaka Castle would be left, the second and third ones would be destroyed. 2. Yodo-dono did not have to go to the Tokugawa Family as a hostage. 3. Instead of that, Ōno Harunaga and Oda Uraku each have to send a person as a hostage to the side of Tokugawa.[439] On

---

437) Ōishi 2020, pp. 203–204.
438) Owada 1997, pp. 196–197.
439) Some information includes one more condition that Tokugawa Ieyasu was not involved with masterless warriors and those of the Toyotomi administration.

December 20th, Ieyasu told both squads to cease fire, sending a commitment form to Yodo-dono and Hideyori in Osaka Castle, and they sending it back to Ieyasu. On the 23rd the peace negotiation was completely established.[440]

The reason why the Toyotomi side accepted not sending Yodo-dono as a hostage to the Tokugawa Family, but instead accepted the destruction of a part of the castle was a courtesy in those days. Although the destruction of a part of the castle was deadly for the Toyotomi side, it implied the meaning of obeying Ieyasu. Yodo-dono and Toyotomi Hideyori followed the manner during the Age of Civil Wars.[441]

However, there were some misunderstandings about landfilling moats around Osaka Castle between the Tokugawa and the Toyotomi's. On December 23rd, the Tokugawa side began to destroy the moats, landfilling not only the outside moat but also the inside one. Yodo-dono soon sent a messenger to Ieyasu, complaining, "This is a breach of contract." Ieyasu understood and accepted what Yodo-dono said, presenting he was going to repair the inside moat. However, it was too late because all the moats were already landfilled and Osaka Castle had lost every defense. The Toyotomi side then got tricked by Ieyasu. Because during Osaka Fuyu no Jin (the Winter Siege of Osaka) Ieyasu was not able to attack Osaka Castle owing to the moats, signing the reconciliation treaty between the two sides was Ieyasu's strategy to landfill all the moats and destroy obstacles to gain Osaka Castle.[442]

Osaka Natsu no Jin (the Summer Seige of Osaka) was now going to begin. Although in March, 1615 Tokugawa Ieyasu received the information that the Toyotomi Family began to produce gunpowder, store rice and lumber, and keep numbers of masterless warriors given gold and silver, Yodo-dono did not

---

440) Owada 1997, pp. 198–199.
441) Fukuda 2007, p. 222.
442) Kuwata 1958, pp. 151–153. Generally, Kuwata's statement has been accepted but recently other evidence states, "Both the Toyotomi and the Tokugawa sides agreed to landfilling both the outside and inside moats. However, because the Toyotomi administration began to dig them up, the Tokugawa side thought of breaking the reconciliation treaty and Osaka Natsu no Jin (the Summer Sige of Osaka) occurred. (Kasaya Kazuhiko 200, pp. 239–241)

98

know that Ieyasu received such information. She sent Ieyasu her messenger to congratulate him on the marriage of his nineth son as they still kept a good relationship on a superficial level. However, on March 15th, Toyotomi warriors set fire to Kyoto. The Toyotomi side excused that they were innocent but Ieyasu did not trust them, saying, "The Toyotomi Family must leave Osaka Castle and move to Yamato, as of now Nara Prefecture or Ise, in the current Mie Prefecture. Or they must let go of the warriors they have." Ieyasu knew that the Toyotomi side did not accept either of them. Yodo-dono answered, "We can't move from Osaka to another place." but she did not tell him anything about letting go of the warriors.[443]

Tokugawa Ieyasu almost decided to begin the war. In April, Ieyasu, Hidetada, his son, Yodo-dono's youngest sister's husband, and a few close confidents had a secret meeting to talk about attacking Osaka Castle in Nijō Castle, Kyoto. Through Jōkōin, a negotiator of the Winter Siege of Osaka, Yodo-dono's younger sister Ieyasu again asked the Toyotomi side about moving to another place or releasing the warriors. However, there was no answer from the Toyotomi side and warriors from the Toyotomi Family attacked Kōriyama Castle where the Tokugawa's warriors took up their position. Then the Tokugawa's side started a full-scale attack. On May 6th, there were battles in Wakae and Yao, and on the 7th in Tennōji and Okayama, with many Toyotomi warriors being killed.[444]

Finally, on the evening of May 7th, the Tokugawa Army was almost ready to attack Osaka Castle and a bloody intense fight was going to happen there. Although Yodo-dono and Toyotomi Hideyori tried to kill themselves in donjon, a trusted vassal pacified them, taking them to the storehouse to hide among the rice husks, where they spent a night. Another trusted vassal released Sen, Hideyori's wife, a granddaughter of Tokugawa Ieyasu from Osaka Castle in order to ask Ieyasu to save Hideyori. However, the Toyotomi side did not get

443) Owada 1997, pp. 201–203.
444) Owada 1997, 203–204.

the answer they expected. The morning of May 8th came. At first there were 500-600 subordinate warriors but then only twenty-eight people were there. Around noon Tokugawa's warrior shot a gun toward the storehouse. It was enveloped in flames and Yodo-dono and Hideyori killed themselves there. Yodo-dono was in her forty-seventh year, Hideyori being in his twenty-third year, and the Toyotomi Family entirely vanished away with Osaka Castle.[445]

---

445) Owada 1997, p. 208.

Conclusion

In conclusion, the work is going to examine whether the three women, Hōjō Masako, Hino Tomiko, and Yodo-dono, are *akujos* (bad women) based on the criteria of twenty-first century Japan, including why and when they came to be called *akujos* after reviewing brief historical backgrounds of each person.

Hōjō Masako

In the late Heian Era (794 – 1185), the Heiji War started in 1159 and Taira no Kiyomori, a boss of the Heike Family in western Japan, defeated Minamoto no Yoshitomo, a head of the Genji Family in eastern Japan. It was a heyday in Taira no Kiyomori's time, the power of the Heike Family covering all of Japan, and Minamoto no Yoshitomo was killed, the Genji Family moving into a decline.

Hōjō Masako was born in 1157 as a daughter of Hōjō Tokimasa taking the Heike Family's side, a local strong man in Izu, the present Shizuoka Prefecture in Japan, although her mother is not clearly known. In 1177 she got married to Minamoto no Yoritomo being relegated to Izu, the third son of Yoshitomo, ignoring the objection of her father. However, after Masako gave birth to a baby girl, Ōhime in 1178, Tokimasa changed his mind and came to have a good relationship with Yoritomo, supporting Yoritomo as his senior subordinate warrior.

Before Yoritomo married Masako, he already had a wife and a baby boy. However, they were separated, the baby being killed because of the strong objection of the wife's father. Her father was very loyal to the Heike Family.

In 1180, Yoritomo received an order from Mochihitoō, the third son of the emperor Goshirakawa. He was told to destroy the Heike Family, and so by and by he decided to attack the Heikes. Although the army of Yoritomo sometimes struggled with the wars, at last he came back to Kamakura, his base, with many warriors who wanted to assist him.

In Kamakura, he built his residence, and Tsurugaoka Wakamiya, where Guardian gods for Kamakura warriors were enshrined, in 1181. Before long Masako delivered a baby boy, Yoriie in 1182, a girl, Sanman in 1186, and another boy, Sanetomo in 1192. Although Yoritomo was very mindful of Masako's healthy deliveries, he never stopped relations with concubines because of his background in Kyoto, where polygamy was common. However, polygamy was never allowed in her district and she ordered her warriors to destroy the residence where his mistress was hidden. After that, Yoritomo again and again had mistresses, and every time Masako grew enraged.

The movement of Kiso Yoshinaka gave Yoritomo a chance to claim victory in the war between the Genjis and the Heikes, extending his power. Kiso Yoshinaka, who had already defeated the Heike Families in the Hokuriku area, decided to fight with the Heike Families in Kyoto. However, he failed in establishing a good relationship with the emperor Goshirakawa, attacking him. Because of this, Yoritomo sent his army to Kyoto in order to save the emperor. After killing Yoshinaka, the army rescued the emperor and moreover, beat the Heike members in the current Hyōgo, Shikoku, Kyūshū and finally Yamaguchi Prefectures. The battle between the Genjis and the Heikes was over in 1185 and the result was the Genji's victory. Yoritomo founded the Kamakura Shogunate and he was assigned as *seiitaishogun* by *chōtei* in 1192.

For a while Masako and Yoritomo had a happy life but they lost their two daughters in 1197 and 1199. Regarding Ōhime, the oldest daughter of Masako and Yoritomo was sick after her fiancé, Minamoto no Yoshitaka, a son of Yoshinaka, was killed. Although after Yoshitaka's death they tried to help her marry a nobleman, she rejected it, saying, "If I have to enter into a marriage,

I'm going to kill myself." In 1195 they also tried to send in Ōhime to the harem of the emperor, Gotoba, to have the emperor's baby. However, the fragile daughter passed away in 1197 before entering the harem in spite of monk's prayers for her recovery. After Ōhime passed away, they again tried to send Sanman to the harem of the emperor, Gotoba. However, she also breathed her last breath before entering the harem. Ōhime was an unhappy princess because her short life was always used to keep good political relationships going by following Yoritomo's social position that was getting higher and higher.

What's more, an unhappy affair happened to Masako, which was Yoritomo's death. In January, 1199 he gasped his last breath probably after falling from a horse. She grew terribly depressed in deep sorrow and she entered a nunnery.

Although after Yoritomo's death, Yoriie, the eldest son between Masako and Yoritomo, succeeded Yoritomo's position, he was not capable as a leader. Masako always supported Yoriie when he was devoting himself to playing *temari* ball, cleaning up his messes and establishing the collegial system with thirteen senior warriors in order to prevent Yoriie from the punishings of an arbitrary government. Later he was very sick and in critical condition. Then an internal territorial battle between the Hōjō family and the Hiki family where his wife was from occurred. Since the Hiki family tried to murder Hōjō Tokimasa, Masako's father, it was destroyed, Yoriie's first son being also killed. Masako had Yoriie become a Buddhist priest and sent him to a temple in the present Shizuoka Prefecture. Yoriie sometimes sent a letter to Masako, telling her his wanton requests. Masako then declined to receive letters from him. Finally, the fragile Yoriie crossed the river when he was in his twenty-third year.

After Yoriie's death, Sanetomo, the second son between Masako and Yoritomo, took over Yoriie's position. He liked to study and was good at composing the *waka* (Japanese poetry). He chose to marry a daughter of a court noble from Kyoto. Again, an internal battle occurred. Maki no Kata, a second wife of his grandfather, Tokimasa plotted to kill Sanetomo who was staying in her home, because she wanted her daughter's husband to become a shogun. As a result, her daughter's husband was killed. Since Tokimasa was always an order-taker of his young second wife, Maki no Kata, without thinking much of politics, Masako sent him to Izu after he became a Buddhist priest. In January, 1219, a cruel event happened. Sanetomo was murdered by Yoriie's son at a shrine when he was in his twenty-eighth year.

The Kamakura Shogunate needed to decide the next shogun as soon as possible because Sanetomo had no heir. Although the government would like to have had someone from the Imperial Family in Kyoto, it was not able to successfully negotiate with the grand emperor, Gotoba.

Then Fujiwara no Mitora (later Yoritsune), the third son of Fujiwara no Michiie, one of the highest court aristocracies, was decided to be the next shogun. At that time Mitora (Yoritsune) was only in his second year.

Because all of the lineal descendants of Minamoto no Yoritomo died, the grand emperor, Gotoba, who had aimed at imperial restoration since before, tried to kill Hōjō Yoshitoki, a regent of the Kamakura Shogunate after his father Tokimasa's death. Because the order was from the grand emperor having absolute authority in Japan, some warriors in the shogunate were reluctant to take the government's side. However, Masako's speech persuaded everyone to fight with the army of the grand emperor as one. In May of 1221, Jōkyū no Ran (the Jōkyū War) broke out. An intense fight was developed and finally the shogunate overcame chōtei.

After the death of Hōjō Yoshitoki, Masako's brother, a regent of Kamakura Shogunate always supporting Yoritomo and Masako, an internal trouble happened again. Yoshitoki's second wife and her brother plotted to get rid of Hōjō Yasutoki, a regent, after his father Yoshitoki passed away, having her real son become a regent. In this case when Masako caught their plot, she immediately solved the trouble without going to war.

At last Masako, who got a lot of jobs done for the Kamakura Shogunate, was sick and departed this life in 1225 when she was in her sixty-nineth year.

After her death, many people with deep grief became Buddhist priests. She was a person who was loved and respected by a lot of people during her life and after her death.

Hino Tomiko

Hino Tomiko, a pretty girl, was born of her mother, Kitakōji Mitsuko, and her father, Hino Shigemasa, in the existing Kyoto Prefecture in 1440. She came from a middle-class noble family, marrying Ashikaga Yoshimasa, the eighth shogun of the Muromachi Shogunate at the age of sixteen. The Ashikagas assumed the acceptance of girls from the Hino family as wives as a custom from generation to generation since Yoshimitsu, the third shogun, received his wife from the Hino family with great success. Hino Shigeko, having authority towards the shogunate, and a mother of the seventh and eighth shoguns, chose Tomiko as Yoshimasa's legal wife.

When Tomiko married Yoshimasa, he already had some intimate friends who had born his three daughters. Imamairi was his favorite friend because she had taken care of him as his nanny. He trusted her very much. She then used her influence with Yoshimasa to interfere with the politics. After their marriage, Imamairi impeded their married life by sending attractive girls to him so that the girls and Yoshimasa spent nights together.

When almost four years had passed since Tomiko and Yoshimasa's marriage, Tomiko finally carried his child. However, the child died soon after its birth. Tomiko, Shigeko, and others related to the Hino family started a rumor that Imamairi had cast a hex on it in order to kill the child, by which she was exiled to Oki Island in Shiga Prefecture. She then killed herself there, holding a grudge against Tomiko and Shigeko. Later, people suffered from several huge natural disasters, and both Tomiko and Shigeko became sick due to, people said, Imamairi's curse. After Shigeko passed away, Tomiko started to become involved into political life as well.

Although Yoshimasa loved only refined pleasures and entertainments, not being interested in politics, he always considered his son and heir. Tomiko and his concubines gave birth to some children but they were all girls. Then he remembered his younger, half-brother, Gijin. He was a Buddhist monk. Yoshimasa asked Gijin to come back to the secular world and take over his place. At first, he did not agree with Yoshimasa as it was still possible for Tomiko to conceive a baby boy. After much prodding, Gijin accepted his request with the promise that Yoshimasa would send any future baby boy to a temple to become a monk. Gijin then changed his name to Yoshimi after leaving the temple. Hosakawa Katsumoto became his guardian.

However, after that, as was feared, Tomiko and other mistresses birthed boys. Tomiko ordered her inner circle to banish all of the mistresses and their baby boys. At last, she had their son as an heir in 1465. He was named Yoshihisa. Yamana Sōzen was chosen as his guardian. Although Tomiko and Yoshimasa were happy, Yoshimasa had mixed feelings owing to Yoshimi's presence. Tomiko very much wanted Yoshihisa to become the next shogun and Yoshimasa then regretted having asked Yoshimi to become his successor.

Down the road, the Ōnin War (1467 – 1477) occurred. The head of the Eastern Squod was Hosakawa Katsumoto, and that of the West was Yamana Sōzen. A power struggle between Katsumoto and Sōzen, and disputes over the successions of the Shiba family, the Hatakeyama family, and the Ashigaka Family were connccted with complexity. Because of their private advantages, they betrayed their friends and were betrayed by them in turn. After both Katsumoto and Sōzen passed away, the war spanning eleven years was finally over. However, a clear result on which side won was never reached.

Throughout her life, Tomiko made strong efforts to multiply her fortune. Before the Ōnin War, she began to lend out money to warriors and the court nobility with high finance charges. During the war, she collected money for both her favors and her curses. The war then allowed her to generate prodigious wealth. She also collected great amounts of taxes from pawn shops and liquor stores, moving on the speculative buying of rice by using this resource. What's more, she later came to manage the money from passenger taxes of seven entrances in Kyoto. She then ran a loan sharking business and amassed a personal fortune by utilizing the public domain. Thanks to her enormous fortune, she continued to increase in power.

After the Ōnin War, Ashikaga Yoshihisa, who had been allowed to assume Yoshimasa's position during the war, grew to adulthood and became a great young shogun. Because Rokkaku Takayori did not obey his orders, Yoshihisa decided to fight with him in order to kill him. The war continued for a long time. Since he only had fragile health, he wound up collapsing on the battlefield. Soon he fell into a serious condition and unfortunately, died in his twenty-fifth year. Tomiko managed his funeral spending about one hundred million yen.

After the death of Yoshihisa (Yoshihiro) and Yoshimasa, Tomiko controlled the shogunate anew. She urgently needed to decide on the next shogun because her young son Yoshihiro did not leave an heir. Yoshiki then became a shogun under her protection. However, because he went around her, ignoring and working against her, she worked with Hosokawa Masamoto to dispatch him through a coup. Finally, Ashikaga Yoshizumi came in as the eleventh shogun. She adopted him and had some say in the politics as his mother and guardian.

Around the age of fifty-five, Tomiko started to recede from political life, no longer insisting on her opinions nor giving strong influence to the shogunate. But she still had a great amount of money. Three months after she and the emperor, Gotsuchimikado, got together to enjoy a ball game in 1496, her health collapsed, she went into a coma, and gasped her last. This was in her fifty-seventh year.

108

Yodo-dono

Yodo-dono (1569 – 1615) was an unlucky lady of fine breeding, a niece of Oda Nobunaga. Her mother was Ichi, a sister of Oda Nobunaga, and her father was Azai Nagamasa. She had two younger sisters Hatsu and Gō who contributed to the *samurai*[446] government in Japan later on. Her name in the days of her childhood was Chacha.

Oda Nobunaga (1534 – 1582), Chacha's uncle from Owari, the current Aichi Prefecture, was the first great *daimyō* (a feudal lord) who led to unify the whole country in Japan after the Ōnin War (1467 – 1477). In 1560, in Okehazama no Tatakai (the Battle of Okehazama), he defeated the Imagawa army that had warriors of about ten times more than the Oda squad with a surprise attack. In order to make his territory larger and obtain authority later on, he helped Ashikaga Yoshiaki become the fourteenth shogun. While he was a great warrior, winning one after another, he was also a person of culture, loving the *chanoyu* (tea ceremony), *sumō* (Japanese-style wrestling), and especially a new weapon, guns. The unification of the whole country was near at hand for him but unfortunately, he was attacked by his subordinate warrior, Akechi Mitsuhide, committing *hara-kiri* in a temple.

Azai Nagamasa (1545 – 1573), Chacha's father, was a *daimyō* in the northern part of Ōmi, the existing Shiga Prefecture, playing an active part in Norada no Tatakai (the Battle of Norada) in 1560. Although in time to come, Nagamasa married Ichi, Nobunaga's sister to keep a good relationship between the Oda family and the Azai family, the alliance between the two was broken, he killing himself when assaulted by Nobunaga.

Ichi, Chacha's mother, was the most beautiful lady during the Age of Civil Wars. She obediently accepted a political marriage with Azai Nagamasa that worked out very well, as their love was true. After Nagamasa's death, she

---

446) *samurai* = warriors

and her three daughters, including Chacha, were rescued and sent back to Oda Nobunaga, living in the home of Nobunaga's brother. After Nobunaga's death, she got married to Shibata Katsuie, Nobunaga's senior subordinate warrior and the relationship between the two was good as well. However, power broking between Katsuie and Hideyoshi occurred and Katsuie was defeated by Hideyoshi, falling on his sword in his castle in 1583. Ichi killed herself with Katsuie, the three daughters being saved and sent to Hideyoshi's armed camp.

At the age of four she lost her biological father, and again she lost her biological mother and father-in-law at the age of fourteen. Then there was no information about Chacha until she became Hideyoshi's secondary wife, giving birth to a baby boy in 1589.

There is no information talking about Chacha's sentiment that she became Hideyoshi's concubine although some of her relatives were killed, which related to Hideyoshi. Hideyoshi seemed to love Chacha since she was similar to Ichi, whom he had romantic notions of for a long time. After the deaths of her mother and father-in-law, Chacha and her two sisters lived in Hideyoshi's residence where they lived a gorgeous and luxurious life with first class food, clothing, and so forth. She might think her life was great in his home and gradually was attracted to Hideyoshi with his high position and authority. Actually, none knows the truth.

Regarding Toyotomi Hideyoshi, although there is no exact information describing his birth, some people say that he was born probably in 1537, being from a poor farmer's family or a son of a foot soldier. Hideyoshi was a brilliant warrior and gradually distinguished himself as a subordinate warrior of Oda Nobunaga. After driving Azai Nagamasa into death owing to Oda Nobunaga's order, Hideyoshi was given Odani Castle by Nobunaga, the first time ever becoming a castellan at the age of thirty-six. After defeating Akechi Mitsuhide betraying Nobunaga, he obtained a position of the first-class subordinate warrior in the Oda family and dominated many areas in Japan, finally becoming *kanpaku* and conducting politics with the emperor. Although he had many concubines in addition to his legal wife, Nene, he did not have biological children and was so happy with Chacha's pregnancy.

In March of 1589, Chacha moved from Osaka Castle to Yodo Castle, gorgeously renovated for her delivery. Since that time, she came to be called Yodo no Kata, a person in Yodo or Yodo-dono, Mrs. Yodo. On the 27th of May, 1589, Yodo-dono gave birth to a brilliant baby boy and he was named Sute. Later his name changed to Tsurumatsu. Yodo-dono and Hideyoshi very much cherished their son and from the field of battle Hideyoshi often sent letters to him, always lavishing affection on him. However, unfortunately, Tsurumatsu was frail and in August, 1591 he was very sick, finally passing away although famous doctors were invited to give him medicine in addition to prayers in temples and shrines.

Although in 1591, after Tsurumatsu's death, Hideyoshi decided to move over his position, *kanpaku* to Hidetsugu, his nephew, becoming a *taikō,* Yodo-dono was again expecting, and on the 3rd of August, 1593, delivering a baby boy anew. He was named Hiroi and later he was called Hideyori. Hideyoshi, who wanted Hideyori to take over his position, deprived Hidetsugu of the *kanpaku*, ordering him to become a Buddhist priest and driving him into committing *hara-kiri* after giving him unjustified complaints that Hidetsugu plotted treachery.

Yodo-dono, the biological mother of Hiroi whose father was *taikō*, was treated hospitably and graciously. She came to have bigger power than any other concubines after delivering and was allowed to do anything on own thought with a luxurious life. However, the position of a legal wife was higher than that of Yodo-dono's, even though Yodo-dono gave birth to an heir of the Toyotomi government.

In spring, 1598, Hideyoshi, who began to be sick and was laid up, finally knowing his death was at hand, arranged his will. He chose five *daimyōs* to manage his politics and five of his senior warriors to perform practical tasks to set up the consultation system, asking them, especially Tokugawa Ieyasu and

Maeda Toshiie, to help Hideyori until he grew up, taking over the Toyotomi administration after Hideyoshi's death. On the 18th of August, Hideyoshi crossed the river of death when he was in his sixty-second year.

Although Hideyoshi asked the five *daimyōs* and the five senior warriors from the Toyotomi Family to help Hideyori until he grew up, soon a problem occurred after the death of Maeda Toshiie, contributing to a collapse of this carefully laid and harmonious system of ten people.

After the death of Maeda Toshiie, Tokugawa Ieyasu began to develop his strategies, trying to hold the real power. This was the beginning of the Battle of Sekigahara in 1600 that was a battle related to a split among friends under the Toyotomi administration between isolated Tokugawa Ieyasu and anti-Ieyasu power. On September 15, 1600 the Battle of Sekigahara occurred. Until the early afternoon of the day the whereabouts of the battle were not identified, but in the evening the side of Tokugawa Ieyasu won the day. It was a big war involving all east-west *daimyōs* although it only lasted a day. After the war, Tokugawa Ieyasu became an actual ruler, reigning over the whole nation. Moreover, in February, 1603, Tokugawa Ieyasu was conferred the position of a *seiitaishogun* by *chōtei* and started the Tokugawa Shogunate in Edo, the current Tokyo. This implied the relation of a master (Toyotomi) and a servant (Tokugawa) was reversed.

After Hideyoshi's death, Yodo-dono had to foster Hideyori who was still small, helping his administration as his assistant with Tokugawa Ieyasu's help. Then after the Battle of Sekigahara she had to bring up little Hideyori, managing the Toyotomi administration by herself.

On the 28th of July in 1603, Sen, who was a fiancé of Hideyori, moved to his residence with her servants. She was a granddaughter of Ieyasu and her biological mother was Gō, Yodo-dono's youngest sister. Although actually the Tokugawa Family was not happy with their marriage, it was a promise between Hideyoshi and Ieyasu before Hideyoshi's death. Furthermore, the two mothers, Yodo-dono and Gō, made an effort to complete it so that the Toyomomi Family and the Tokugawa Family kept up a good relationship.

However, Tokugawa Ieyasu tried to conquer the Toyotomi administration, ruling the Tokugawa government. He encouraged Toyotomi Hideyori to give Tokugawa Hidetada words for celebration after Hidetada became a *seiitaishogun.* However, Yodo-dono never accepted it because it implied the Toyotomi Family would become a *daimyō* under the Tokugawa administration. Before long, a matter related to the inscription on a bell at Hōkō-ji rebuilt by Yodo-dono and Hideyori occurred in 1614. Ieysu accused the Toyotomi side falsely, saying that the inscription suggested future misfortune for the Tokugawa government. Because Yodo-dono did not have such a bad intention against Ieyasu, she sent a messenger to Ieyasu to excuse the matter. However, they were not able to negotiate peacefully and on November 26, Osaka Fuyu no Jin (the Winter Siege of Osaka) started. Owing to the hard battle, Ieyasu considered a peaceful settlement. However, there were some misunderstandings about landfilling moats around Osaka Castle between the Tokugawa side and the Toyotomi one. Because the Tokugawa side began to destroy the moats, landfilling not only the outside moat but inside one as well, Yodo-dono soon sent a messenger to Ieyasu, complaining, "This is a breach of contract." But it was too late and Osaka Castle lost every defense. Yodo-dono was tricked by Ieyasu. Because of another unjustified complaint from Ieyasu, Osaka Natsu no Jin (the Summer Siege of Oasaka) began. The Tokugawa army defeated the Toyotomi side one by one. Finally, around noon on May 8, 1615, Tokugawa's warrior shot a gun at the storehouse where Yodo-dono and Hideyori were hiding. The storehouse was enveloped in flames and they killed themselves there, the Toyotomi Family then entirely vanishing away with Osaka Castle. Yodo-dono was in her forty-seventh year and Hideyori was in his twenty-third year.

Here the paper describes how the three women influenced their governments in order to examine whether they were *akujos*. First, we'd like to see what they did. They had a job in common. It was Shinto and Buddhist affairs. When their husbands were alive, they covered the job together and continued it after their deaths.

For example, regarding Hōjō Masako, both publicly and privately visiting temples and shrines together was a common event for Masako and Yoritomo, though after his death she had to do it by herself. She related with Buddhist and Shinto services that were usually held by the shogun. It was her main job. On every New Year's Day she took part in events associated with Shinto and Buddhist deities with Yoritomo. Moreover, in October, 1185 when a service for completion of work in Shōchōjuin (a temple) built by Yoritomo in Kamakura was held, Masako took her seat at the temple's right side and Yoritomo took his at the left side.[447] After having children, they visited shrines and temples with them.

Regarding Masako's independent visit, whenever Yoritomo went to a war front, she prayed for him in temples and shrines with her servants. On the 10th of August, she paid her respects at Tsurugaoka Hachimangū with her female servants to pray for Yoritomo's victory of the Battle of Ōshū[448] occurring in the current Tōhoku district. This continued from July to September in 1189. In January, 1194 she visited shrines at Izu and Hakone in order to make presents of various things.[449] It was an important event and basically, it was the shogun's job held on every new year, which presented his authority. Masako did the shogun's job instead of him. It means that she had the same power as Yoritomo had.

What's more, Masako established temples and ordered Buddha statues and Buddhist paintings. In February, 1200 she chose land in Kamegayatsu[450] where a temple[451] would be set up and ordered Eisai[452] to manage the temple.[453]

---

447) Nomura 2000, pp. 40–45. Gomi & Hongō 1, March, 2008, p. 143.
448) Gomi & Hongō 20, September, 2008, p. 100.
449) Gomi & Hongō 10, April, 2010, p. 39.
450) Kamegayatsu is in Kamakura.
451) Its name is Kikokusanju Fukukingō Zen-ji. (亀谷山寿福金剛禅寺)
452) He was also called Yōsai (1141–1215), a famous monk in the Kamakura Era.
453) Gomi & Hongō 10, June, 2009, p. 146.

Kamegayatsu was a place where Yoritomo tried to live at the time he came into Kamakura after the battle. In addition, Ōhime's grave was near here and the residence of Yoshitomo, Yoritomo's father was there.[454] The shogunate reared Daiji-ji[455] and on the 27th of July, 1214, a Buddhist service was held which she attended. Apparel and horses were devoted.[456] According to *Azumakagami*,[457] the article of the 15th of October, 1222 talked about the Buddha statue she received. She also seems to receive Buddhist paintings from famous Buddhist painters in Kyoto and Nara.

Hino Tomiko also visited temples and shrines, spending a lot of money on them. For instance, Tomiko paid her respects at Isejingū (a shrine), in the current Mie Prefecture with many people forming a line on the 14th of September, 1479 and in April, 1484. The event was very gorgeous, which represented her imposing financial power and many people gathered to watch it.[458] Isejingū was a shrine of the highest rank in Japan and located at the top of all the Japanese shrines. It was managed and maintained by the *chōtei* and shogunate governments until World War II (1941–1945). Amaterasu Ōmikami, a guardian goddess for royal families and all Japanese people is enshrined there and, people say, she grants all kinds of wishes. In Japanese mythology, she was said to have established the Japanese nation.

What's more, in June, 1481 Tomiko visited Katsuragawamudō-ji located in the present Shiga Prefecture with her son, Ashikaga Yoshihisa, to pray for his success as a shogun because the temple held a statute of the Goddess of Kannon that was popular among people at that time and Tomito also believed in it.[459]

Furthermore, in August, 1481, Tomiko imposed the rebuilding of Kōsui-ji established in 1156 – 1159 on the people in Yamanashishichigō, the current

454) Seki 2004, pp. 192–193.
455) 大慈寺
456) Gomi & Hongō 10, April, 2010, pp. 8–10.
457) Gomi & Hongō 10, November, 2010, p. 9. (*Gendaigoyaku Azumakagami*)
458) Tabata 2018, p. 139, pp. 188–189.
459) Tabata 2018, pp. 179–180.

Yamanashi Prefecture.[460] On the 12th of September, fifty-two laborers were
working, on the 15th thirty-six, on the 16th thirty-six, on the 17th twenty-one, and
on the 18th fifteen, so a total of 160 laborers were working on the job.[461]

In 1483, Tomiko donated a lot of money for the building of a subordinate
shrine on the grounds of the Yoshida Shrine in Kyoto. Yoshida Shrine was
said to have been built around 859 – 876, though it was not clear, and Yoshida
Kanetomo inaugurated Yoshida Shintoism during the Muromachi Period, with
authority in the field. In 1442, she also donated some money to the shrine for
its repair. Yoshida Shrine seemed to receive good protection from her.[462]

Regarding Yodo-dono's Shinto and Buddhist affairs, the paper already
described some in the text and the affairs presented were briefly summarized.
In 1589, she held a memorial service for her biological parents, Azai Nagamasa
and Ichi, and in 1594 Nagamasa's twenty-first anniversary of death. After
Hideyoshi's death she spent a lot of money for the building and repairing of
shrines and temples under the name of Toyotomi Hideyori. Hideyoshi started
to establish the shrines and temples, with Hideyori taking them over after
Hideyoshi's death. Beginning in 1598, almost a hundred temples and shrines
were rebuilt and repaired. For example, in 1601, the main hall of Yamato
Hōkadō, in the current Nara Prefecture was rebuilt, and in 1602, the chapel
of Ōmi Ishiyamadera, now in Shiga Prefecture was renovated. Yodo-dono
was a devout believer in Buddhist and Shinto deities. Moreover, in 1607,
because Kōdaiin asked Hideyori (Yodo-dono) to set up the Kitano Shrine in
Osaka, it was built. She also constructed a new bridge in Keikōin, the existing
Mie Prefecture, because the former bridge was destroyed by a fire in 1601.
She deeply took care of the temple because in days of old the Azai family
financially supported it, too. Finally, she rebuilt Hōkō-ji that became a cause of
the destruction of the Toyotomi Family.

---

460) Tabata 2018, p. 180.
461) Tabata 2018, p. 186.
462) Tabata 2018, pp. 187–188.

Here the author would like to give a glimpse of the cultural background at that time in Japan. In those days, people seemed to very much believe in gods.[463] People often visited temples and shrines[464] to keep the government stable, prevent natural disasters and diseases, to pray for safe delivery and travel, pray for victories in war, etc.

Furthermore, according to the information about the age of Hōjō Masako, people seemed to trust what diviners said. They may have thought the diviners were mediators between the gods and them. Masako and the people at the Kamakura Shogunate sometimes invited the diviners and received their divinations. Between the late Heian Period and the early part of the Kamakura Period, if a fortune-teller said, "Because it is an unlucky day today, you should cancel the appointment of work," people canceled the appointment and most of them accepted the cancel, understanding the reason why it was made void. Moreover, if an augur prophesized, "That direction is dire," people went to their destinations in a wide circle, avoiding that direction. What's more, around that time people recognized dreams as oracles. For instance, on 29th of February, 1202 Masako had a dream of Yoshitomo, Yoritomo's father, which the paper discussed a little above, and in her dream he said, "I want you to move my old house to the temple in Kamegayatsu that you began to build in 1200." Because of this dream, Masako followed what he told her and moved his house to Kamegayatsu to use his house as a chapel.[465] In addition, on March 22, 1221 when the Jōkyū War occurred, she received a message from a shrine in her dream. It presented, "Although from now on the world is going to be at war, Yoshitoki would be able to pacify it after contributing to the shrine." Masako trusted the message and contributed to the shrine.[466]

Regarding the period of Hino Tomiko, people believed that casting a hex was absolutely effective. After the first baby between Tomiko and Yoshimasa

---

463) Japan accepts the polytheistic religion, therefore, people believe there are many gods.
464) At that time Christianity was not yet popular in Japan.
465) Gomi & Hongō 10, November, 2009, pp. 21–22.
466) Gomi & Hongō 10, April, 2010, pp. 101–102.

passed away, a rumor was circulated that the baby had been killed because Imamairi and her acquaintances had called down a curse upon the baby. They asked a monk to pray for the baby to die. Tomiko used the rumor and told it to Yoshimasa. He became very angry and had Imamairi arrested, sending her to Oki Island near Lake Biwa in the present Shiga Prefecture and finally she killed herself. People thought that it was natural for her to receive some form of punishment.

Moreover, back in those days, people seemed to believe in the deep connection between people in another world and people who were still living. They believed that a person who died as a victim exacted revenge after their death. After Imamairi breathed her last, the most bizarre phenomena appeared in Kyoto. People became afraid of natural disasters, saying that they were Imamairi's haunting. What's more, Tomiko was very afraid of Imamairi's curse, holding a service for Imamairi, because her father's aunt, Shigeko suddenly grew sick and died. (Though now few people in Japan think much of this.)

When it comes to the Age of Yodo-dono, people seemed to believe the connection between spirit people and living people. In 1589, she held a memorial service for her biological parents, Azai Nagamasa and Ichi, and in 1594, Nagamasa's twenty-first anniversary of death as the paper mentioned above. Holding their service and anniversary implies that she still connected with them, as if they were still existing somewhere close to her, hoping for their happy lives after their deaths. Although the custom is still carried out in Japan, it is not paid much attention to as it used to be.

When someone became sick, people often visited temples and shrines to pray for their recovery. For instance, Tsurumatsu, the first baby boy between Yodo-dono and Hideyoshi, was frail, and whenever Tsurumatsu was in serious condition, some people asked priests in temples and shrines to pray for his recovery. However, unfortunately, he died at last. Around 1593, smallpox became prevalent and unluckily, Yodo-dono was affected by the disease. Bcause Hideyoshi was concerned about her very much, he ordered all temples and shrines in Japan to pray for her recovery and gave large rice donations. Around that time, although doctors existed, medical science was not so advanced and people seemed to entirely depend on praying in temples and shrines.

Let's go back to the original subject about how they contributed to their governments.

Masako was busy with not only Buddhist and Shinto affairs but politics as an *amashogun*. After Yoritomo's death, Masako supported the Kamakura government helping young Yoriie, Sanetomo, and Yoritsune in various aspects. She often made an effort in order to prevent internal battles. For example, when Yoriie took Adachi Kagemori's secondary wife and tried to kill Kagemori, Masako sat down with Yoriie, talked to him about his unreasonable act, and persuaded Yoriie not to kill Kagemori. Moreover, she visited Kagemori's residence and recommended him to write a letter discussing his innocence to Yoriie. At the time, Hiki Yoshikazu, Yoriie's father-in-law tried to murder Hōjō Tokimasa, Yoriie's grandfather, because of a disagreement of territory distribution. Masako soon got information of the murder and told it to Tokimasa. Although Tokimasa hit Yoshikazu, they were able to prevent a war. In the event that Hōjō Yoshitoki's second wife and her brother, Iga Mitsumune, plotted to get rid of Hōjō Yasutoki and have her real son, Hōjō Masamura become a regent, Masako asked Miura Yoshimura to work it out with Iga Mitsumune. As a result, they did not have a big internal battle.

Masako had the authority of dividing territories to her subordinate warriors especially after Sanetomo died, which was one of the shogun's jobs. The important rule of the Kamakura Shogunate was the master and servant system. It was a feudal society. While the servants loyally served their master, working for their master at the risk of their lives, the master gave them rewards, especially territories, based on their achievements. They had to fight with enemies, protecting their master with their lives. The connection between the two was very strong like a family. They served their master, protecting their territories that were given by their master after keeping him safe with their lives. In those days, territories given by masters were very significant and meaningful for them. Masako was therefore respected and thought much of by her warriors as their master.

In addition, Masako very much worked for the shogunate. After Sanetomo's death she got in touch with *chōtei* in Kyoto in order to find the next shogun. At the time of the Jōkyū War, her powerful speech helped her warriors become as one and led a victory of the shogunate. Again, there were no women making such a speech in those days and even now, it is conveyed as a legend in Japanese history. She was then a necessary person for the Kamakura government at that time in history.

Regarding Hino Tomiko, her control of the government was inevitable for the society of that time. Yoshimasa was not interested in politics, devoting himself to entertainment, and Yoshihisa (Yoshihiro) was too young to manage the government. It was Tomiko who needed to work for the shogunate. Most of all, the selection of the shogun is significant because the shogunate doesn't work without him. After the death of her husband and son, she urgently needed to decide on the next shogun because her young son Yoshihiro did not leave an heir. After Yoshiki, and then Yoshizumi were chosen by her, Ashikaga Yoshizumi finally came in as the eleventh shogun. She adopted him and had some say in the politics as his mother and guardian. Since she thought so highly of the shogunate, she put herself in service to it.

What's more, throughout her life, Tomiko made strong efforts to multiply her fortune and generated prodigious wealth. As it relates to Tomiko's ability to increase financially, it was great, inasmuch as she learned from her brother. She spent a lot of money generously on what was just. For example, she donated a good deal of money to affairs related to the imperial palace, the emperor's court, and court nobles who lost their homes in a fire during the Ōnin War.[467] She also made contributions to many temples and shrines burned in the war. In addition, she gave generously to Buddhist monks and other people. Furthermore, she invested her money into the shogunate. In a way, her money almost equals that of the shogunate. In other words, she rebuilt Muromachi Shogunate's finances instead of her husband who was unable to do that, and she ended the war. Importantly, during and after the war, there were lots of people who were saved by her. For instance, she spent a lot of money to help warriors of the Western army without financial resources to withdraw from Kyoto at the end of the war, which implies she contributed to have the war end.[468] It was Tomiko who put a period on the war. Without her advanced financial acumen, the war would not have been able to come to an end. In actual fact then, she was not a "*shusendo*".

When it came to Yodo-dono, as well as Masako and Tomiko, she came to have involvement with politics after Hideyoshi's death. She also needed to foster Hideyori who was still small, helping his administration as his assistant with Tokugawa Ieyasu's help. Then, after the Battle of Sekigahara, she had to manage the Toyotomi administration by herself, bringing up Hideyori who never reached adulthood.

Furthermore, Yodo-dono had to take on the household management, including Hideyoshi's huge inheritance property, spending a lot of money for repairing and building shrines and temples under the name of Toyotomi Hideyori.

In order to maintain a good relationship between the Tokugawa Family and the Toyotomi one with Gō, she made an effort to complete the marriage between Hideyori and Sen whose biological mother was Gō and biological grandfather was Ieyasu.

Finally, although she and Hideyori killed themselves at Osaka Castle, that was enveloped by flames through the attack of Ieyasu's army, she tried to

---

467) Tabata 2018, p. 122.
468) Tabata 2018, p. 125.

protect the Toyotomi administration until the last.

Tabata talks about the tasks of widows in the world of warriors during these eras. The relationship between husband and wife was almost equal,[469] and the widow supported the 'family' (government) as a head with supreme command after the death of her husband.[470] She enjoyed decision-making influence on choosing a successor and having to take responsibility for the successor, bringing one up until it grew up.[471] Moreover, she needed to divide territories[472] and the most important job was to carry out Buddhist affairs.[473]

After checking the tasks of widows at that time, discussed by Tabata, we recognize that the three women seemed to work very hard to accomplish their jobs aiming to protect their governments and be 'not bad'. Then why are they called 'akujos'?

Here the paper is going to review how modern people in Japan think about these three women: how they are atroucious. Ōya mentions in *Hōjō Masako* written by Nagai Michiko,[474] "People said that Masako was an *akujo* because she possessed a jealous nature, a strong desire for political power, etc." According to Torigoe[475], Hino Tomiko is said to have had a jealous nature too, and brought down the Ōnin War. What's more, Tabata heard that Tomiko generated prodigious wealth, running a loan sharking business and a rice business in Kyoto.[476] Some people assert that she was a miser. Regarding Yodo-dono, Kuwata pointed out that her high pride finally destroyed Oasaka Castle and the Toyotomi administration.[477] What the paper mentioned above has been talked about publicly from long ago.

---

469) Tabata 2003, p. 186.
470) Tabata 1994, pp. 98–99; Tabata 1998, p. 251.
471) Tabata 1994, p. 97.
472) Tabata 2003, p. 195.
473) Tabata 2003, p. 189.
474) Nagai 2021, p. 589.
475) Torigoe 2000, p.107.
476) Tabata 2018, p. 1.
477) Kuwata 1958, pp157–158.

122

However, here are some critical acclaims about the women discussed by some people who knew the circumstances in those days.

For example, Masako's reputation was fine at the time she passed away. For example, *Azumakagami* describes that she was a good woman that everyone loved, likening her to a great female politician in China and Japan.[478] Since she ordered her subordinate warrior to destroy the residence where Yoritomo's mistress was hidden, she might be called a person with a jealous nature. However, it is a kind of convention people were familiar with in those days and we should not call her an *akujo* due to this.

Regarding her strong desire for political power, she needed to manage the government after the deaths of Yoritomo, Yoriie, and Sanetomo because at that time, it was common for the wife to take over her husband's work in the warrior's world. A respected Buddhist priest, Jien who was older than she by two years, supported the political activities of women in those days. Moreover, Ichijō Kanera, a court aristocrat also affirmed them in discussing female emperors and a female god in ancient Japan in his work, *Shōdanchiyō*.[479]

Sanjō Nishi Sanetaka (1455 – 1537) who was a court aristocrat, neither poked fun at Tomiko nor criticized her, on the other hand, saying that she should be respected by people.[480]

Because it is a historical fact that Tomiko ostracized Yoshimasa's mistresses one by one, people say she had a jealous nature. However, in the twenty-first century, monogamy is absolute and there are many women that agree with her. Moreover, we have no problem suing the husband's girlfriend(s) for 'consolation' money. Owing to people's way of thinking now, Tomiko is not an "*akujo*".

As the paper already mentioned, Tomiko did not catalyze the Ōnin War but rather put a period to the war. Without her advanced business and financial

---

478) Gomi & Hongō, 10 November, 2010, p. 60. (*Gendaigoyaku Azumakagami*)
479) Nomura 2000, pp. 140 and 151.
480) Tabata 2018, p. 207.

sense, the war would not have been able to reach a timely end. In actual fact then, she was not a "*shusendo*".

Because Yodo-dono was a niece of Oda Nobunaga, a wife of Toyotomi Hideyoshi, and a mother of Hideyori, she was not able to allow herself to follow Ieyasu's request and the Toyotomi government was destroyed by Ieyasu. If she had followed his request, the government might not have ceased to exist. This is what Kuwata wants to say.   However, his opinion is too big a leap as there is no evidence that the administration was ended by her.   We should rather consider that, as a result, the administration happened to disappear even though she tried very hard to protect it.

Now let's look at their actual conciliatory and female behaviors.

Masako helped and took care of women who were in egregious situations during the wars because they had no relationship with the wars that men conducted.   For example, she conferred a favor to Miyagiku, a younger sister of Kiso (Minamoto no) Yoshinaka, killed in Kyoto in 1184.   When Miyagiku was set up and falsely accused of a crime, Masako saved her.[481]   Furthermore, regarding Shizuka, Yoshitsune's secondary wife, Masako was nice to her, too. Shizuka was a famous and talented singer and dancer.   In 1186, she was taken to Kamakura although she said she did not know where Yoshitsune was.   In Kamakura, Masako and Yoritomo asked her to show them her dance.   However, Shizuka declined, saying that she was sick.   They again insisted that she do so, so she danced and sang a song implying the sadness of parting with Yoshitsune, attaching herself to him.   Yoritomo was angry asserting, "I don't like the song because it includes her love toward Yoshitsune, a traitor against me."   However, Masako understood Shizuka and soothed him, reminding him about their love story when Masako's father had made her marry someone, and she had run away from her husband into a shrine at Izu Mountain to see Yoritomo in torrential rain.   Then he came off his high temper and Masako gave a reward to

---

481) Gomi & Hongō 1, March, 2008, p. 81.

Shizuka.[482] Masako always stood up for the disadvantaged and watched over them.

Tomiko helped Ashikaga Yoshimi's daughter make her way into a Buddhist nunnery as a disciple of a famous nun. Tomiko took her to the nunnery as her adopted child since the daughter relied on Tomiko for support. Although Yoshimi was her opponent during the Ōnin War, she was nicely looked after as a member of the Ashikaga Family.[483]

Someone states that Yodo-dono had a gentle nature, helping people around her. According to Rekishijō no Jinbutsu.com and History land,[484] she asked Ieyasu to invest in masterless warriors and gave a lot of money as livelihood assistance to Nobunaga's mistress who was short of cash. She also built a temple, Yōgenin, for her mother and father. As we know that her maids gathered before her grave at the anniversary of her passing to create a memorial service for her, we understand that she was a good-natured person and loved by them.

Then when did people begin to call the three women 'akujos'? According to Ōninki[485] talking about the Ōnin War, written in the late Muromachi Era (1336 or 1338 – 1573), and based on the ideas of Confucianism emphasizing hierarchical society and women's inferiority, it says that the cause of the Ōnin War was Tomiko. Yoshimasa, a Shogun not being very good at politics, should have left his job to a mature shogunal deputy but he left it to Tomiko, a young woman without education or sound political judgement. Because of this reason, Japan devolved and the war occurred. The author of the book blamed not only Tomiko but other women controlling and managing the government.

In the Edo Era (1603 – 1686), especially in essays written by male writers

482) Gomi & Hongō 20, June, 2008, pp. 40–42.
483) Tabata 1998, pp. 16–17.
484) Rekishijō no Jinbutsu.com 2021, Rekishi wo Wakariyasuku Kaisetsu! History Land.
485) Shimura 2017, p.12. The author used Ōninki transcribed into modern Japanese, Gendai Goyaku Ōninki. The writer of the original book is unknown.

and presented not based on historical fact but on people's way of thinking and the trend of the world in Japan at that time, Hōjō Masako and Yodo-dono also were described as terrible women. For example, Hōjō Masako was a nymphomaniac, relating with Hatakeya Shigetada (her subordinate warrior), Minamoto no Sanetomo (her son), and Hōjō Yoshitoki (her brother). Although there are no written materials discussed the evidence, the writer says, these stories are transmitted by word of mouth. In the middle of the Edo Period, an essay represented that Yodo-dono's wrong brought down the demolition of the Osaka Castle. Moreover, another essay mentions that the Toyotomi administration was destroyed because Yodo-dono was too erotic, relating with men other than Hideyoshi.[486] Again there are no writings talking about the events, although there were some rumors that two sons that Yodo-dono gave birth to were not Hideyoshi's children.

The auther would now like to sidetrack, taking a look at the cultural background associated with women's social position in Japan. According to a Japanese myth, the world was created by a female god and in ancient Japan, the women's position was even higher than men because the woman gave birth to children. In the Heian Era (794 – 1185 or 1192), marriage in aristocratic society was mainly the wife's father arranging the daughter's husband, offering them their residence. This means that the couple lived with the wife's parents. At that time women's social status was still high, almost the same as that of men. In the Kamakura Period (1185 – 1333) the lifestyle of marriage changed and the couple came to live in the husband's house. After the Kamakura Era, the warriors' period, women's social position was getting lower because women did not fight with armory. People began to think that the stronger gender, men with big power, were superior. However, the women's social status was not so terrible, as it was after the Edo Era. In the Edo Period the Tokugawa Shogunate accepted Neo-Confucianism, whose ideas were to build up a hierarchal pyramid

---

486) Ōtsuka 2019, p. 84.

126

of social forms.[487]

Around that time, people were gradually accepting a male-centric society and came to think that women were inferior to men. Polygamous society was common and men were allowed to have mistresses. On the other hand, women were not allowed to do so and the importance of their chastity was emphasized. Women were obliged to be gentle, sincere, obedient, and never be jealous. Women working as well as men was not demanded by the Japanese government. Because of these policies, women's status became very low and in the warrior's society the wife had to obey her husband completely, being required to be gentle, sincere, and obedient. It was denied that women related to politics and denied that a husband even talked to his wife about it.[488] In the early years of the Meiji Period (1868 – 1912), it looked like the new world would contribute to the women's status but it was in vain. Since the Edo Shogunate continued for more than 260 years, it was difficult to change people's way of thinking. In the Meiji Period, the Japanese government stated that men were outside workers and women belonged inside to do homemaking, childrearing, and following and supporting their husbands. In the 1960s when Japan began to recover from the defeat of World War II, the idea based on Confucianism came back.

After reviewing the Japanese cultural background and women's social status in each period, we can recognize that the three women's reputation associates with them. Before the Edo Period, men and women were still almost equal although the position of women in society was slowly getting lower. At that time people neither requested women to be gentle and obedient nor to just follow their husbands lead. Masako especially was born in the Heian Period when men and women had equal social status. She was not a lady without having any authority, just meekly following her husband with all the reins of power. In the time she was alive, her behaviors were acceptable and nobody

---

487) Actually, it was a Japanese Confucianism based on the Chinese one. Japanese Confucianism (Shushigaku) was more strict and artificial, exerting great pressure upon individuals.
488) Nomura 2000, p. 154.

blamed her. She had a right to know what Yoritomo knew, not only about the politics but every affair that happened in the shogunate, and a right to provide directions to their subordinate warriors. Masako and Yoritomo shared almost anything associated with public affairs. It was common for the wife to take over her husband's work in the warrior's world and that her reputation was good, people praising her saying, "She was a great female politician."

On the other hand, during the Tokugawa Shogunate in the Edo Period when the Japanese government denied women's political participation, obliging women to be gentle, sincere, obedient and never be jealous, and emphasizing the importance of their chastity, the three women's reputations were reversed. First, they were politicians. People then did not accept female politicians because in the Edo Era, women were prohibited to associate with politics. People looked at them as women being intrusive and without womanly decency. Moreover, Tokugawa Shogunate requested women to never be jealous. However, Masako and Tomiko never allowed their husbands to have mistresses, ostracizing the mistresses one by one and burning the house where the mistress lived. Because of this, people might have had a bad impression of them seeming them as harsh, strong women with a fighting instinct. Although the Tokugawa government also insisted that women keep their chastity, there had been pervasive rumors of adultery for Tomiko and Yodo-dono: Tomiko with an emperor, Yodo-dono with Hideyoshi's subordinate warriors, though there is no clear evidence about either. Because of this, young Yodo-dono might be described as a nymphomaniac woman, not being satisfied with old Hideyoshi at night.

In the Edo Period, women were educated to be self-effacing and not to insist on their opinions, completely following their husbands in Japan. What's more, academic education for women was frowned upon and people believed that women were much the inferior to men. It was absolutely out of the question for women to act in public and control politics side by side with men. The three women definitely protruded from the ideal woman at that time.

128

Because of this, it seems that in essays and fiction they were easy targets for gossip and called terrible women based on creations then when print technology was developed. If they were obedient and quiet ladies, they wouldn't have left their names in Japanese history until now.

Regarding Yodo-dono, according to Owada[489], she was described as a dreadful woman by historians supporting the Tokugawa Shogunate then because they needed to beautifully and affirmatively present the process that the Tokugawa Shogunate was destroying the Toyotomi administration. Since the historians had to emphasize Tokugawa Ieyasu's justice, it was necessary for them to represent her as an awful woman. Because Ieyasu broke his promise that he was going to help Hideyori until he grew up, taking over the Toyotomi administration after Hideyoshi's death, he needed just cause for destroying the government. What he wanted to say was that he destroyed the administration since Yodo-dono was wrong.

In the introduction of the work, another name of Yodo-gimi is introduced. As the work already mentions, gimi implies the meaning of a prostitute, although the name was familiar with people in Japan now. The name might be pushed by the people taking the side of the Tokugawa government in those days in order to make her seem a dreadful woman.

When we examine the three women based on the female criteria that the Tokugawa government decided on using Japanese Confucianism, they might be ostracized women. In the Meiji Period and in the 1960s when Japan began to recover from the defeat of World War II, the idea based on Japanese Confucianism came back. Although the status of Japanese women now is much better and less hard than that of the Edo Period, the government coming to announce gender equality and female participation in politics, it is sure that there are still some people, especially old ones keeping the idea of Japanese Confucianism and not accepting outstanding women. Their awful reputations

489) Owada 1997, p.170.

seem to have pervaded and come to stay during the Edo Period, sustaining more than 260 years and continue up to today without revision.

When we examine the three women based on criteria in the twenty-first century in Japan, they are not bad women but brilliant female politicians. Regarding Masako, it is not too much to say that the Kamakura Shogunate, the first warrior's government, was opened and established the foundation of the warrior's government subsequently continuing for almost 700 years by uniting two cooperating people, Masako and Yoritomo sharing the same purpose, though there were a lot of subordinate warriors helping them. After overcoming the deaths of Yoritomo and her four children, she managed the government as an *amashogun*. If she had been a well-bred young lady without any hard experiences born in Kyoto, she would not have been able to do very much to help Yoritomo and contribute to the Kamakura Shogunate. Masako with her large capability was needed when the Japanese nation changed a lot.

When it comes to Tomiko's excellent business and financial abilities, in spite of being uncommon and difficult to be accepted by people of the day, she helped many people, putting a period on the Ōnin War and protecting the Ashikaga government. She was a great politician, not a *shusendo* at all. Although as a result, Yodo-dono was not able to keep the Toyotomi administration, she actually had no intention of destroying it. Kuwata says that if she had accepted Ieyasu's requests that helped the Toyotomi administration, the Toyotomi Family might not have disappeared.[490] However, she did not receive the mercy of the enemy, which was the warriors' gracious attitude in those days. Although she was not a warrior, she understood the warrior spirit and fought with their creed to the death. She was a brave politician. It was up to her the way forward, whether she followed Ieyasu or not, and she made her choice so we should respect it.

Nowadays, women's taking part in politics is encouraged in the world,

---

490) Kuwata 1958, pp. 161–162.

although Japanese women are still not so positive about it. The Global Gender Gap Report states every year that the number of Japanese women participating in society is small, and women's social position has not yet improved. Women's entry into politics is promoted, however. The twenty-first century modern society of Japan seems to demand dynamic and active women like Hōjō Masako, Hino Tomiko, and Yodo-dono. In the final analysis, then, they are not *akujōs* at all but women to be admired.

References

Azusawa Kaname. "Rekishi ni Manabu Josei Katsuyaku (Dai 2 Kai) Tachibaniyotte Tsukurareta Amashogun Hōjō Masako." *Jinzai kyōiku: HRD Magazine* 29: 10: 346 (October, 2017): 74-77.

Azusawa Kaname. "Rekishi ni Manabu Josei Katsuyaku (Dai 5 Kai) Gametsui Akujo ka Jiritsu Shita Onnaka Hino Tomiko" *Jinzai Kyōiku* (January, 2018): 74-77.

Dōmon Fuyuji. "Rekishi wo Tsukutta Joseitachi (2) Hino Tomiko Tatakau Onna Shogun "*Uzushio* 539 (January, 2004): 276-281.

Dōmon Fuyuji. "Rekishi no Naka no Sōmu Buchō (367) Hino Tomiko (3) Posuto Yoshimasa wa Dareni？ "*Shūkan Sōmu* 53, 12, 646 (December, 2015): 58-61.

Dōmon Fuyuji. "Rekishi no Naka no Sōmu Buchō (379) Hino Tomiko (15) Tairan Sankasha ni Yūshi Suru " *Shūkan Sōmu* 54, 12 (December, 2016): 58-61.

Dōmon Fuyuji. "Rekishi no Naka no Sōmu Buchō (380) Hino Tomiko (16) Nihon Mecha Kucha ni Naru" *Shūkan Sōmu* 55, 1 (December, 2017): 58-61.

Emiya Takayuki. "Minamoto no Yoritomo【Zenpen】～ Heike Datō wo Nashitogeta Genji no Onzōshi." *Rekishijin*

Fukuda Chizuru. *Yodo-dono: Ware Taikō no Tsuma to Narite.* Mineruba Shobō, 2007.

Fukuda Chizuru. *Toyotomi Hideyori.* Kabushiki Kaisha Yoshikawa Kōbunkan, 2014.

Gomi Fumihiko & Hongō Kazuto. *Gendai Goyaki Azuma Kagami 1 Yoritomo no Kyohei.* Kabushiki Kaisha Yoshikawa Kōbunkan, 10, November, 2007.

Gomi Fumihiko & Hongō Kazuto. *Gendai Goyaki Azuma Kagami 2 Heike Metsubō.* Kabushiki Kaisha Yoshikawa Kōbunkan, 1, March, 2008.

Gomi Fumihiko & Hongō Kazuto. *Gendai Goyaki Azuma Kagami 3 Bakufu to Chōtei.* Kabushiki Kaisha Yoshikawa Kōbunkan, 20, June, 2008.

Gomi Fumihiko & Hongō Kazuto. *Gendai Goyaki Azuma Kagami 4 Ōshū Gassen.* Kabushiki Kaisha Yoshikawa Kōbunkan, 20, September, 2008.

Gomi Fumihiko & Hongō Kazuto. *Gendai Goyaki Azuma Kagami 5 Seiitaishogun.* Kabushiki Kaisha Yoshikawa Kōbunkan, 10, March, 2009.

Gomi Fumihiko & Hongō Kazuto. *Gendai Goyaki Azuma Kagami 6 Fuji no Makigari.*

Kabushiki Kaisha Yoshikawa Kōbunkan, 10, June, 2009.

Gomi Fumihiko & Hongō Kazuto. *Gendai Goyaki Azuma Kagami 7 Yoriie to Sanetomo*. Kabushiki Kaisha Yoshikawa Kōbunkan, 10, November, 2009.

Gomi Fumihiko & Hongō Kazuto. *Gendai Goyaki Azuma Kagami 8 Jōkyū no Ran*. Kabushiki Kaisha Yoshikawa Kōbunkan, 10, April, 2010.

Gomi Fumihiko & Hongō Kazuto. *Gendai Goyaki Azuma Kagami 9 Shikken Seiji*. Kabushiki Kaisha Yoshikawa Kōbunkan, 10, November, 2010.

Gomi Fumihiko & Hongō Kazuto. *Gendai Goyaki Azuma Kagami 11 Shogun to Shikken*. Kabushiki Kaisha Yoshikawa Kōbunkan, 10, February, 2012.

Hatakeyama Hiroshi. "Tokushū: Hino Tomiko to Muromachi no Ningengaku Ashikaga Yoshimasa – Ginkakuji Zōei ni Shūchaku Shita Kenryoku Naki Shogun – Seijiryoku wa Sofu Yoshimitsu ni Tōku Oyabazu, Kenseiyoku suramo Tsuma Tomiko ni Oyobanakatta ga" *President* 32, 4, (April, 1994): 74-79.

Honda Asajirō. *Nihon Rekishi Kōgi Jōkan, Kaitei Zōho 8 Han*. Kanasashi Hōryūdō, 1913.

Itō Jun. *Shura no Miyako*. Kabushiki Kaisha Bungei Shunjū, 2021.

Izawa Motohiko. "Gyakusetsu no Nihonshi (339) Randa no Teiō Ashikaga Yoshimasa Hen (6) Yūjūfudan na Shogun to Tsuma Hino Tomiko no Wagamama ga Maita Tairan no Tane" *Shūkan Posuto* 31, 22, 1492 (June 11, 1999 a): 120-123.

Izawa Motohiko. "Gyakusetsu no Nihonshi (351)Hino Tomiko to Kairai Seiken Hen (2) Kyoto ni Tsukurareta Shichikō no Sekisho no Nyūjōryō wo Ōryō Shita Gōyoku Buri" *Shūkan Posuto* 31, 35, 1505 (September 10, 1999 b): 96-99.

Izawa Motohiko. "Gyakusetsu no Nihonshi (353)Hino Tomiko to Kairai Seiken Hen (4) Otto Yoshimasa to Musuko Yoshihisa – Shogun no Shigo mo Otoroenai Hino Tomiko no Kenryoku no gensen" *Shūkan Posuto* 31, 38, 1508 (September 24, 1999 c): 96-99.

Kaionji chōgorō. "Akunin Retsuden (9) Hōjō Masako." *Ōru Yomimono* 16 :7- 16 :12 (1961): 318-341.

Kasaya Kazuhiko. *Sekigahara Gassen to Osaka no Jin*. Kabushiki Kaisha Yoshikawa Kōbunkan, 2007.

Kobayashi Chigusa. *Yodo-dono: Sengoku wo Shūen Saseta Onna*. Yōsensha. 2011.

Kuwata Tadachika. *Yodo-gimi*. Kabushiki Kaisha Yoshikawa Kōbunkan. 1958.

Mitani Masao. *Hyōden Hino Tomiko*. Mainichi Shimbunsha, 1994.

Miyamoto Yoshimi. "Sekigahara Gassen no Daimondai-Toyotomi Hideyori wa Naze

Shutsujin Shinakattanoka" *Rekishi Dokuhon* 44(8), 709,1999: 164-169.

Mori Miyoko. "Josei Hen Hino Tomiko VS Imamairi no Tsubone – Muromachidai de Arasou Shogun Yoshimasa Seishitsu to Aishō" *Rekishi to Tabi* 23, 17 (November, 10, 1996): 370-373.

Nagai Michiko. *Hōjō Masako.* Kabushiki Kaisha Bungei Shunjū, 2021.

Nomura Ikuyo. *Hōjō Masako Ama Shogun no Jidai.* Kabushiki Kaisha Yoshikawa Kōbunkan, 2000.

Ōishi Manabu. *Issatsu de Wakaru Sengoku Jidai.* Kawade Shobō Shinsha. 2020.

Ōtake Masayuki. "Hōjō Tokimasa Kō: Minamoto no Yoritomo, Hōjō Yoshitoki • Masako tono Kankei wo Chūshin ni." *The journal of Kamakura Women's University* 25 (2018) : 166-158.

Ōtsuka Hikari. "Jokeizu de Miru Nihon Sōranshi (Dai 10kai) Sekigahara no Kassen • Osaka no Jin Yodo-dono Akujo Setsu no Dedokoro." *Nami* 53(5) =593 (2019) : 84-91.

Owada Tetsuo. *Sengoku Sanshimai Monogatari.* Kadokawa Shoten, 1997.

Rekishi wo Wakariyasuku Kaisetsu! History Land https://history-land.com/yododono/ (Accessed 6 January 2023).

Rekishijō no Jinbutsu.com https://colorfl.net/yododono-seikaku/, 2021 (Accessed 6 January 2023).

Seki Yukihiko. *Hōjō Masako.* Kabushiki Kaisha Mineruva Shobō, 2004.

Shimura Kunihiro. *Gendaigoyaku Ōninki.* Kabushiki Kaisha Chikuma Shobō, 2017.

Tabata Yasuko. "Chūsei Josei no Eikō to Jitsuzō – Hōjō Masako to Hino Tomiko" *Tachibana Joshi Daigaku Kenkyū Kiyō* 13 (1986): 71-99.

Tabata Yasuko. *Nihon Chūsei Josei Shiron.* Hanawa Shobō, 1994.

Tabata Yasuko. *Nihon Chūsei no Shakai to Josei.* Kabushiki Kaisha Yoshikawa Kōbunkan, 1998.

Tabata Yasuko. *Bakufu wo Seotta Amamidai Hōjō Masako.* Jimbunshoin, 2003.

Tabata Yasuko. "Kamakura Otto wo Erabitotta Amashogun –Minamoto no Yoritomo to Hōjō Masako." *Rekishi Dokuhon* 55:10 (October, 2010): 92-97.

Tabata Yasuko. *Muromachi Shogun no Midaidokoro Hino Yasuko • Shigeko • Tomiko.* Kabushiki Kaisha Yoshikawa Kōbunnkan, 2018.

Takahashi Hideki. *Chūsei no Ie to Sei.* Kabushiki Kaisha Yamakawa Shuppansha, 2004.

Takano Noboru. *Kenryoku wo Nigitta Onna- Hōjō Masako, Hino Tomiko, Yodo-gimi, Kasugano Tsubone.* Kabushiki Kaisha Shufunotomosha, 1978.

Torigoe Midori. "Tokushū Nihonshi 2000 nen no Josei Emaki-Joseishi 2000 nen Josei wo Meguru Jiken Ōnin no Ran <Hino Tomiko> *Rekishi Dokuhon* 45, 1, 716 (January, 2000): 106-109.

Watanabe Tamotsu. *Hōjō Masako*. Kabushiki Kaisha Yoshikawa Kōbunkan, 1961.

Yabe Kentarō. "Sekigahara no Tatakai to Tenka no Yukue: Kita no Mandokoro to Yodo-dono no Kanyo" *Rekishi Dokuhon* 59 (11) = 905, 2014: 85-88.

Yoshida Tomoko. "Oichi no Kata Nobunaga no Imōto." *Rekishi to Tabi*, 23, 8, 1996: 192-197.

"Nihon Sandai Akujo? Yodo-dono no Seikaku Towa" Rekishijō no Jinbutsu.come: https://colorfl.net/Yododono-seikaku/: 2021/04/28 (Accessed 22 October)

"Yodo-dono no Seikaku ya Akujo to Yobareta Riyū towa? Yodo-gimi no Imi mo Kaisetsu." History Land: https:history-Land.com/yod

Author's Profile

IIDA Yoriko
Adjunct Lecturer at Osaka Metropolitan University

M.Phil. Teachers College, Columbia University, USA
M.A. University of Missouri, St. Louis, USA
B.A. Konan University, Japan

OMUP

大阪公立大学出版会（OMUP）とは
本出版会は、大阪の5公立大学－大阪市立大学、大阪府立大学、大阪女子大学、大阪
府立看護大学、大阪府立看護大学医療技術短期大学部－の教授を中心に2001年に設立
された大阪公立大学共同出版会を母体としています。2005年に大阪府立の4大学が統
合されたことにより、公立大学は大阪府立大学と大阪市立大学のみになり、2022年に
その両大学が統合され、大阪公立大学となりました。これを機に、本出版会は大阪公
立大学出版会（Osaka Metropolitan University Press「略称：OMUP」）と名称を改め、
現在に至っています。なお、本出版会は、2006年から特定非営利活動法人（NPO）と
して活動しています。

About Osaka Metropolitan University Press (OMUP)
Osaka Metropolitan University Press was originally named Osaka Municipal
Universities Press and was founded in 2001 by professors from Osaka City
University, Osaka Prefecture University, Osaka Women's University, Osaka
Prefectural College of Nursing, and Osaka Prefectural Medical Technology College.
Four of these universities later merged in 2005, and a further merger with Osaka
City University in 2022 resulted in the newly-established Osaka Metropolitan
University. On this occasion, Osaka Municipal Universities Press was renamed to
Osaka Metropolitan University Press (OMUP). OMUP has been recognized as a
Non-Profit Organization (NPO) since 2006.

Three Notorious Female Politicians
in Feudal Japan

2024年5月31日　発行

著　者　　飯 田　依 子（IIDA Yoriko）

発行者　　八 木　孝 司

発行所　　大阪公立大学出版会（OMUP）

〒599-8531　大阪府堺市中区学園町1－1

大阪公立大学内

TEL　072(251)6533

FAX　072(254)9539

印刷所　　石川特殊特急製本株式会社